The Complete Book of
Home Winemaking

H. E. Bravery

The Complete Book of Home Winemaking

Pan Books London and Sydney

First published 1970 by Arco Publications
Reprinted 1971 by MacGibbon & Kee Ltd for Arco Publications
This edition published 1973 by Pan Books Ltd,
Cavaye Place, London SW10 9PG
4th printing 1977
© H. E. Bravery 1970
ISBN 0 330 23503 6
Printed and bound in Great Britain by
Hazell Watson & Viney Ltd, Aylesbury, Bucks

CONTENTS

INTERNATIONAL CONVERSION TABLES

These conversion tables are intended to help all users of Pan books – wherever they live in the world. The weights and measures used throughout this book are based on British Imperial standards. However, the following tables show you how to convert the various weights and measures simply.

International Measures

Measure	UK	Australia	New Zealand	Canada
1 pint	20 fl oz	20 fl oz	20 fl oz	20 fl oz
1 cup	10 fl oz	8 fl oz	8 fl oz	8 fl oz
1 tablespoon	$\frac{5}{8}$ fl oz	$\frac{1}{2}$ fl oz	$\frac{1}{2}$ fl oz	$\frac{1}{2}$ fl oz
1 dessertspoon	$\frac{2}{5}$ fl oz	no official measure		—
1 teaspoon	$\frac{1}{5}$ fl oz	$\frac{1}{8}$ fl oz	$\frac{1}{6}$ fl oz	$\frac{1}{6}$ fl oz
1 gallon	160 fl oz	160 fl oz	160 fl oz	160 fl oz
$\frac{1}{2}$ gallon	80 fl oz	80 fl oz	80 fl oz	80 fl oz

Conversion of fluid ounces to metric

1 fl oz	= 2·84 ml
35 fl oz (approx 1$\frac{3}{4}$ Imperial pints)	= 1 litre (1000 ml or 10 decilitres)
1 gallon (160 fl oz)	= 4·800 litres
$\frac{1}{2}$ gallon (80 fl oz)	= 2·400 litres
$\frac{1}{4}$ gallon (1 quart)	= 1·200 litres
1 Imperial pint (20 fl oz)	= approx 600 ml (6 dl)
$\frac{1}{2}$ Imperial pint (10 fl oz)	= 300 ml (3 dl)
$\frac{1}{4}$ Imperial pint (5 fl oz)	= 150 ml (1$\frac{1}{2}$ dl)
4 tablespoons (2$\frac{1}{2}$ fl oz)	= 70 ml (7 cl)
2 tablespoons (1$\frac{1}{4}$ fl oz)	= 35 ml (3$\frac{1}{2}$ cl)
1 tablespoon ($\frac{5}{8}$ fl oz)	= 18 ml (2 cl)
1 dessertspoon ($\frac{2}{5}$ fl oz)	= 12 ml
1 teaspoon ($\frac{1}{5}$ fl oz)	= 6 ml

All the above metric equivalents are approximate

Conversion of solid weights to metric

2 lb 3 oz	= 1 k (kilogram)
1 lb	= 453 gm (grammes)
12 oz	= 339 gm
8 oz	= 225 gm
4 oz	= 113 gm
2 oz	= 56 gm
1 oz	= 28 gm

FOREWORD

Before you start I should point out that the home-made wines made by our grandparents have been greatly improved upon in recent years: we hundreds of thousands of amateurs are busy making wines that compare so well with commercial products that only the most discerning palate is able to detect the difference.

Commercial firms are now making and marketing them at roughly eight to ten times what it would cost you to make them for yourself: surely nothing more needs to be said to prove how worthwhile really good home-made winemaking is today.

It never ceases to amaze me that no sooner has my latest book appeared with its immensely wide range of recipes that one imagines would cover enough recipes and ideas to last anybody a lifetime, than I receive numerous letters by every post, requesting recipes for wines I was sure had lost their popularity.

Sometimes the writer hints vaguely that he wants to make 'a kind of Sauternes-flavoured Riesling'; the ideas some people get hold of are beyond me. Then readers of my magazine articles all come wanting something apart from what I have given them. However, I am grateful to them because they let me know what people want.

Although I have evolved hundreds of recipes, many of which have now become world-renowned, and modified many more, so that in all my books put together there must be at least seven to eight hundred different ones, there are still countless people wanting something different.

The most surprising and interesting point about this is that, despite the popularity of ready-prepared ingredients such as concentrated grape juices, special flavourings which enable us to make vermouth and other wines flavoured of world-famous liqueurs, pre-packed dried elderberries, bilberries, sloes and other dried fruits, all of which can make top quality wines, most people who write to me wish to use the same ingredients as did our grandparents – but they still want better wines. One possible explanation is that while the ready-prepared ingredients make excellent wines, they are inclined to cost a little more; it could well be that many regard the ready-prepared stuff as being somewhat like dehydrated soups with which anybody, however stupid, can make soup, whereas a truly interested wine maker, when he has made good wines, wishes to claim that he has done it all himself, forgetting about the man who evolved the recipe and the method. So this book has become necessary in the hope that my readers will find recipes here for whatever type or variety of wine they would like to make.

Chapter 1

INTRODUCTION

There must be over a million serious winemakers in this country alone. There are many millions more in America, Canada, New Zealand, Australia and many other parts of the world where my books are read. They work to simple fool-proof methods to make a very wide range of top-class wines. With their experience they know what they have to use and do to make the type and variety of wine they want and they do it with the sure knowledge that it will turn out just as they wanted it. And that is as it should be.

Unfortunately, there must be millions of others jogging along with practically no idea of what they are doing except that they are following a recipe. It never occurs to them to ask whether it is any good or not. I come across them every day. People who let their wines ferment of their own accord, that is, without added yeast, so that wild yeast and bacteria are able to set up some sort of fermentation that will turn out a concoction that these unfortunate people are somehow able to liken to wine. But these points and many others are fully covered in later pages.

The trouble is that many people still imagine that in this enlightened age all home-made wines are make-shift inferior products and there is nothing that can be done about it.

This is the worst that anybody could think, for the truth is that well-made home-made wine, made with a good recipe and method, and a bit of common sense on the part of the hobbyist, is as good and often better than commercial products costing a pound a bottle.

Indeed, many people well known in public life, as well as retired businessmen, doctors and service commanders not only make their own wine but also entertain guests with them. They could not do this if their wines were not top rate. And you can do the same.

It is all a matter of using a good recipe with a sensible method and then being sensible throughout. Put your mind to it (without worrying) and you will make wines the like of which you always thought were beyond you.

But you will not do it if you have previously made wines with old recipes and antiquated methods and still want to use part of these with part of mine.

You must forget about those. You must also forget what Granny or Mum told you and what they used to do. You must start with a clean sheet, an open mind and the readiness to learn the basis of a few simple principles of what is relatively a simple subject.

If you do this you will be in for a lifetime's pleasant hobby in which the rewards are probably greater than most others.

This does not mean having to use expensive utensils and apparatus. Nor does it mean that you will have to learn all about the scientific and chemical aspects. Nevertheless, you may have to throw out the old bread crock you may have been using together with any other dangerous utensils you may have. It will also mean that you will not float the yeast on toast any more. Nor will you 'pop the corks in for a week or two'.

As will be seen in later pages these ideas are as out-dated as the Ark and the cause of more disappointments than anything else.

But you will not regret starting anew, for when you open your first bottle after six months you will have the most delightful surprise of your life.

Chapter 2

WHAT SORT OF WINE SHALL I MAKE?

I have been making wines for over thirty years and know with certainty that if everybody setting out to make wines for the first time were to ask themselves this simple question, instead of making the first wine that comes into their head, there would be far fewer disappointed beginners.

But the fact is that too many have heard that 'such and such' makes a good wine or that 'my uncle Fred used to . . .' and away they go without giving any real thought to the type of wine the ingredients will make or whether they will like it or not. Later, they wonder what went wrong with 'such and such' or whether 'my uncle Fred' was off his nut or not.

I have even known people to buy a good book on the subject and work a recipe without reading any of the factual information a good book contains: what is often worse is that they get two or three books each by a different author and then follow part of the directions of one, switch to the directions of the second and then finish off with the directions of the third.

What this sort of person fails to realize is that when a writer on this subject has evolved a recipe he has also evolved the method that goes with it. Therefore, his directions are the best to follow simply because he has worked it all out and tested it in consideration of how the various ingredients react. For example, one set of instructions will suffice a large group of fruits but go outside that group and the instructions must be varied to suit. This applies in many different ways when making wines. So do stick to one author and do consider carefully which type of wine you are likely to appreciate most.

Be especially careful about making them sweet, medium

sweet or dry. I say this because a large number of people *think* they like dry wines when in fact they do not. But not until after they have made a really dry wine do they realize it. The same applies to sweet wines. What those not liking the sweet or dry require is a medium wine but they seem not to realize it in the early stages of their winemaking.

Now, not all ingredients are suitable for making into dry wines any more than others are suitable for making into sweet wines. You will not get a good wine from rhubarb, for example, if you make it sweet. Nor will you get a good dry wine from elderberries unless you are particularly skilled with this fruit. Where possible, I have given a brief description of the type of wine one can expect from each recipe or group of fruits together with the amounts of sugar to use for dry, medium and sweet where, for example, the ingredients being used are suitable for three types of wines. I also make it clear when the ingredients are best used for a sweet wine only, or only for a dry wine.

Naturally tastes vary and for this reason when you have become skilled, as you will quite quickly, you will be able to work off your own bat to suit your individual preferences.

But in any case, your early efforts will be top-rate wines. It really boils down to the fact that the longer you are making wines the greater your preferences develop towards one type – usually the dry sorts. This is because you will slowly develop what we call an educated palate and when this has happened you will be able to manipulate any recipe to make almost any kind of wine you want. Know-how is the thing and you can only acquire this by experience in making a wide variety of wines.

Be this as it may, if you have no previous experience, do use the simpler one-fruit recipes in the early stages as it is with these that you are most likely to be successful at the very first try.

Chapter 3

THE CAUSE OF WINE SPOILAGE AND HOW TO PREVENT IT

This chapter is not designed to deter you. It is designed to show you the stupidity of antiquated methods which take no account of the many reasons for wine being spoiled and to show you how easy it is to prevent this.

Any winemaker who has had any of these problems will at once be given new hope of success – this cannot be described as a deterrent.

Making wines is something like growing plants. It is no earthly use painstakingly raising seeds into small plants and then lovingly planting them into soil in which you have put expensive fertilizers, if you let caterpillars, blackfly, greenfly, slugs and a multitude of other pests destroy them. Similarly it is no use making top-class wines if you let them be ruined by the many diseases lurking in the offing.

It is far less expensive and infinitely easier to combat the diseases of wines than it is to combat a dozen slugs.

All the troubles mentioned are caused by bacteria and wild yeasts, which are ever present in the air, waiting to alight on any material upon which they can live and breed. Fermenting wines, or crushed fruits prepared for winemaking, are an attraction which wild yeasts and bacteria cannot resist, simply because they are ideal breeding grounds in the same way as a piece of meat is to a bluebottle. We all know what happens when a bluebottle attacks meat. There is no need here for a lengthy description of the effects of each disease except to say that they turn wines to vinegar or make them sour, insipid and flat or bitter and cloudy, thick and oily or spoil them irrecoverably in other ways.

Bacteria and the spores of wild yeasts are invisible to the naked eye, but a dangerous germ carrier known (wrongly) as the wine fly can be seen. This is in fact the fruit fly or bacteria fly; a tiny off-white fly to which one would hardly give a second glance. They can be seen in their billions on bacteria beds in sewage plants and often in thousands around damaged fruits. They are harmless in themselves, but they carry many types of bacteria, mainly the vinegar bacteria which converts the alcohol in wines to acetic acid – the main constituent of vinegar. Only one or two will appear while you are making wine or around your fermenting vessel, but one is enough. If not seen and destroyed it will commit suicide in your wine leaving the germs it carries to do their worst at some later stage

Wild yeast and bacteria are also on the very fruits with which we make wines. They are also inside bottles and on corks – indeed, they are on everything we use and they are everywhere where we work when making wines.

At first sight it may appear that we are up against an impossible task when we set out to make wines; but we are not. If we were, there would not be millions already making top-class products.

Wild yeasts and bacteria on the fruits may be disregarded for all intents and purposes because these are destroyed by the methods used. Only where fruits are crushed and left to ferment as instructed by many old methods is there any risk of wild yeasts and bacteria causing the many troubles previously mentioned. It will be seen from this that the old direction to crush the fruits and leave to ferment (without sterilizing in some way or adding yeast) is the main cause of failure. When we set out to make wines by modern methods we destroy all the causes of disease already on the fruits at the outset. All we have to do after this is to keep the fermenting wines covered throughout and sterilize all equipment with an easily prepared solution which costs practically nothing to make up.

Sterilizing Solution

It is wise to make this up when you are about to make your first batch of wine so that you always have it ready. Obtain 2 oz of sodium metabisulphite from almost any chemist and dissolve this in about one pint of warm water. Make sure all is dissolved and then make this up to half a gallon with cold water. As half-gallon jars are not ordinarily obtainable from dealers in home winemaking equipment, it is best to obtain one from a dispensing chemist. Normally they will let you have them at about 8p each.

This solution is known as sulphite solution and is really sulphur dioxide gas in solution. Strong solutions when smelled often give off slightly suffocating odours especially to those suffering from chest ailments. But the strength recommended is not great enough to cause personal discomfort, yet is at the same time quite strong enough to destroy wild yeasts and bacteria on utensils in a trice.

As will be seen in the methods in later pages, wild yeasts and bacteria on the ingredients themselves are destroyed either by a milder solution of sulphite or by heat treatment. So it is only utensils, bottles, etc, that we need bother with at this stage.

The fermentation vessel should be swilled out with about a pint of this solution and then rinsed before the ingredients are put in to be crushed. The used solution is then returned to the jar for future use. Funnels, colanders, straining cloths and suchlike used during the various processes should also be rinsed with this solution before use: straining cloths may be dipped in this, wrung out as dry as possible and then, when unfolded, shaken well before use. The reason for rinsing and shaking the tightly wrung-out straining cloth is that the solution can destroy the yeast we use to ferment our wines. Therefore, if we put fermenting wine into a jar containing only a small amount of this it could halt fermentation and present you with the problem of getting it going again. See *Sticking Ferments* p 32.

It will be seen in the methods that after a time in the fermentation vessel the wine is transferred to jars. These jars, like the bottles the wine will be put into when it is a finished product, must also be rinsed well with this solution. Put about a pint into a jar (about ¼ pint to a bottle), shake it well so that all the inside surface is wetted and then return to the bulk for future use. When sterilizing bottles put the solution in the first bottle, shake as with the jar, then transfer to the next bottle and so on. Having done this to the required number of bottles, put half a pint of cooled boiled water into the first bottle, shake it well, put it into the next bottle and so on until you have rinsed them all. Then stand them upside down while you prepare the wine for bottling.

While you are doing this, the corks can be soaked in some of the solution in a small basin with something heavy on top to keep them submerged. Planned in advance this operation can be completed in a matter of minutes. If you use modern plastic corks which are becoming very popular you need only dip them in the solution before putting them into the bottle. But do shake them free of solution before pressing them home.

Other preventive measures against wild yeasts and bacteria are even more simple. All that has to be done is to cover the fermentation vessel with sheet polythene with no holes in it and to tie this down tightly with strong thin string. If you use a polythene pail, as most of us do for one- or two-gallon lots, it is wise to remove the handle. If this is done, tying down the cover is much easier. If you do not want to do this, a good plan is to put the pail in a polythene bag, gather it up and close it with an elastic band. The gas generated during fermentation can escape easily whichever method is used.

This will keep your wine protected during fermentation. Where daily stirring is involved one merely takes off the cover (or removes the elastic band). After the operation the fermenting wine must be covered again at once.

As will be seen in the methods, after a time, the wine is strained and put into jars. And here we use a fermentation lock to protect our precious products.

The Fermentation Lock

This is a very important part of our equipment and is instrumental in our fight against spoilage bacteria and wild yeasts during the later stages of production. But apart from this important function it also helps us to determine the rate of fermentation and assists in producing an extra 1–2 per cent of alcohol. This it does because it cuts off the oxygen supply to the yeast. The yeast must have oxygen and because it cannot obtain it from outside the jar, as it would if a fermentation lock were not fitted, it turns to the sugar for its supply, thus converting a little more sugar than it might into alcohol.

The fermentation lock is fitted when directed in the methods. Sterilizing solution is then poured in to the level shown and a small knob of cotton wool is lightly fitted into the open end. Fermenting wines under this protection are absolutely safe.

Gas produced by the yeast during fermentation passes through in the form of bubbles and the solution closes up behind them preventing air and the diseases it carries from gaining access. It is wise to examine the lock every week or so because it sometimes happens that the solution dries up when fermentation in the jar remains vigorous. After about a month, the lock should be removed, cleaned and refilled with new solution. If this is not convenient, add a few drops of new solution once a week.

It will be seen when you have your first batch under a fermentation lock that bubbles pass through at considerable speed. But later the frequency diminishes so that after a few weeks the solution remains pushed up on the outgoing side and there appears to be no activity at all. This indicates that fermentation is near its end. But do not interfere with the lock or wine at this stage. Leave well alone until the solution returns to level in the 'U' bend. Even when this has happened it is best to leave the wine for a further two or three weeks just in case fermentation gets going again to produce an important 2–3 per cent more alcohol (see Yeast, Fermentation and the Production of Alcohol, p 22).

These simple precautions against spoilage yeasts and bacteria are no trouble at all when you are making wines because they fit into the general method neatly and effectively. And certainly they prove the senselessness of that oft-read direction to 'pop the corks in loosely for a week or two'.

Utensils

Very little in the way of utensils are needed to start with because most people start with one-gallon lots to get the feel of things before embarking on larger amounts. This is very wise for it allows you to assess which wines you are going to like most and which you do not want to make a second time without having made too much of one sort.

The essentials are a two-gallon rigid polythene pail for fermentation purposes: this we call the fermentation vessel. Colanders and funnels will doubtless already be in the house and these are quite suitable provided they are not of metal or, if enamel, not chipped. If in doubt as to their suitability it is best to buy a polythene colander and funnel and a quart jug with a half-pint and pint graduated scale on it as all these things will come in handy and are unbreakable.

But do make sure all these items are genuine polythene as some plastics are not suitable. The jug can of course be of glass or Pyrex.

You will also need two one-gallon-size carboys or cordial bottles which may be obtained for about 15p each. These are used with the lock fitted for the secondary fermentation stage.

Also needed (but not until halfway through making your first batch) will be a suitable siphoning tube. This may be merely a couple of yards of polythene transparent tubing of about three-sixteenth bore. Attached to this can be a glass tube with the last half-inch of one end upturned but this is not essential. So settle for the tubing to start with and elaborate on your equipment as and when you wish. On no account make it expensive as there is absolutely no need for it.

Only when you have been making wines for a while and decide to make large amounts – say, four- or five-gallon batches – will you need more by way of utensils than I have mentioned.

On no account ferment wines in metal containers, otherwise metallic flavours and toxic substances may find their way into the wines, possibly rendering them dangerous.

Old bread crocks, old barrels of doubtful origin, in fact, any old utensils in previous use, are best not used at all. Many old utensils gave lead into the wines that were made in them, the result being that people suffered lead poisoning as a result of drinking their wines. Modern utensils are cheap, easy to clean, unbreakable and absolutely safe.

Bottles may be bought new but I have found wine merchants and off-licences generous in that they will most likely let you have all you need for nothing. Getting half a dozen at a time in this way soon builds up a useful stock. Wine bottles are, after all, never used twice by the trade simply because it is cheaper to buy new ones rather than pay someone to wash and sterilize used ones.

Corks, especially the new plastic sort, are cheap so there is no need to resort to using second-hand cork ones. These in any case are a risk as the deep pores may harbour spoilage yeasts and bacteria which may not be reached by short soaking in sterilizing solution. Plastic corks will soon supersede the cork-made sort and, as mentioned, these are easy to clean and sterilize, can be used over and over again without losing their shape.

Your own cork-made corks may be re-used if when you remove them from their bottles you wash and soak them in sterilizing solution for a few minutes and then dry them and put them in a polythene bag tied up tightly.

Chapter 4

YEAST, FERMENTATION AND THE PRODUCTION OF ALCOHOL

Without added yeast there would be no fermentation of our fruit mixtures and therefore no wine and no alcohol.

True, if the mixture were left long enough, some sort of fermentation would be set up either by wild yeast or bacteria reaching the mixture and some sort of horrible concoction with perhaps a slightly winey or beery flavour would result.

As will be seen in the methods, we destroy wild yeasts and bacteria on the ingredients before we begin: at the right time we add yeast of the most suitable type to ferment our wines for us (see: *Choice of Yeast* p 27).

When we add yeast to a fruit juice and water mixture either it is in its dormant state or it may have been activated if you have started a nucleus as recommended on p 29.

The first thing to happen is that an enzyme in the yeast inverts the sugar present into two slightly different sugars so that other enzymes present can ferment it. The yeast then begins to reproduce itself – in other words, the yeast begins to breed. Millions of new yeast cells are produced and these live upon the sugar in order to sustain themselves. In doing this they turn approximately half into alcohol and half into the gas we see leaving the wine during fermentation.

In the normal way, up to two and a half pounds of sugar per gallon is the maximum sugar the yeast is able to digest. This is because this amount of sugar produces roughly 15 per cent of alcohol by volume. And this amount of alcohol is the maximum most yeasts are able to tolerate. It follows then that when this amount of alcohol is made the yeast is destroyed by it. When this happens, fermentation ceases and no more alcohol is made.

Fifteen per cent of alcohol by volume is a good percentage, not only from the alcohol content point of view, but because it is sufficient to preserve the wine. There are special yeasts which, under favourable conditions, are able to withstand up to and perhaps just a bit more than 18 per cent but under normal home conditions it is wise not to expect more than 15 per cent.

It certainly seems that in recent years certain strains of yeast are being produced capable of withstanding higher percentages of alcohol. This is understandable when one considers that certain germs which were once quickly destroyed by small doses of certain antibiotics now need much stronger doses. In a similar manner certain yeast strains are becoming able to withstand higher concentrations of alcohol so that one day – not too far off I hope – yeasts capable of making about 20 per cent will be common.

This is not to say that we want all wines as strong as this but it would certainly be helpful where special wine types are required.

On the whole, 15 per cent is enough for most wines and usually too much for dry sorts which are better for being in the region of 10–11 per cent.

But alcohol production is not all that goes on during fermentation. Fermentation, let me add, is a very complex series of enzyme action and interaction about which the average home operator need know nothing at all. This is because if he prepared his recipes well, including all the ingredients in proper proportions, he will have a must (prepared mixture) reasonably well balanced to allow all the actions and interactions to take place almost automatically.

It is during these actions and interactions that esters which help to form the bouquet and the flavour are produced and these are just as important as alcohol. Indeed, I would say, more important because a wine with a mighty kick and precious little flavour is not nearly so good as one with a good flavour, bouquet, roundness and fullness whether it contains a lot of alcohol or not. Warmth during fermentation is of great importance if we are to obtain a constant fermentation that will produce all the constituents that go to make up a good wine.

Warmth ensures that the yeast remains active from the time it begins to produce alcohol until it has made the maximum. Normally a temperature of 65–70°F. (15–20°C.) is ideal but 5°F. either way will not be calamitous. A problem here is often how to keep the wine at a constant temperature when this varies from day to day or even hourly. Many people make themselves what we call fermentation cupboards and fit them with a thermostatically controlled heater for the purpose: the whole thing costs about £1.75. A friend of mine who has recently taken up winemaking has converted an old box otto-man for the purpose and this is ideal. It is just deep enough to accommodate eight one-gallon jars with enough headroom for the fermentation locks when the lid is closed.

The length of fermentation depends on many factors: for example, if a dry wine of 11 per cent of alcohol is being made, fermentation will cease quicker than if a wine containing 15 per cent is the aim because there is less alcohol to be made. Also, when more sugar is present, the action of the yeast is usually a little slower.

Length of fermentation depends too on whether the must is balanced or not. A well-balanced must is one containing a suitable proportion of all the essentials of a good fermentation and these consist mainly of acid, tannin, a certain amount of organic matter such as fruit particles, sugar in reasonable proportions and yeast. Certain elements are also needed but these are usually already there. The recipes in this book are balanced suitably in so far as they can be; however, it is im-possible for anybody evolving recipes to be able to take into account the vagaries of our climate which affect to a certain degree the acid and sugar content of our fruits.

For example, during a good season, fruits when ripe con-tain less acid and more sugar. In a poor season, the reverse is true. Type of soil (acid or otherwise), variety of fruit tree and other factors all bear upon the final balance of the must. We can use chemical apparatus to adjust various chemical matter but this is both expensive and easily broken, besides being difficult to use unless you have laboratory experience. This sort of thing is not for people working in their own kitchens and who will not mind if one batch is slightly different to the next batch made with the same recipe and ingredients. We want good wines with the minimum of expense and worry in manufacture. These can be had quite easily without resorting to chemical analysis and balancing.

It is also doubtful whether a chemically balanced must, checked and rechecked with elaborate equipment, will eventually turn out a better wine that will cease fermenting earlier than one made with a well balanced recipe.

As mentioned, the recipes here are as balanced as they need be for a constant and full fermentation resulting in a well-balanced wine when fermentation is complete. In the normal way fermentation should cease in about eight to twelve weeks from the time it begins. It could end sooner and it could go on a bit longer, so do not imagine something wrong if yours does not behave exactly as you think it should.

The adding of sugar in stages is important from the point of view of full fermentation although it does tend to lengthen fermentation by a week or two. However, this does not matter because if a lot of sugar is added at the start or if too much is added at any stage, there is a risk of fermentation stopping before the maximum alcohol is reached. When this happens it is very difficult to get fermentation on the go again. The result is that you have a lower alcohol wine than you want with more sugar left unfermented than you aimed at and such a wine is liable to be attacked by one of the many diseases already mentioned.

Racking – transferring wine from one container to another – also reduces the rate of fermentation to a certain degree, but this must be done, otherwise 'off' flavours may be given into the wine by dead yeast cells and decaying vegetable matter (fruit particles) at the bottom of the vessel.

The reason racking slows down fermentation is that when this operation is carried out some of the active yeast is left in the vessel but this cannot be helped. In any case, there is enough yeast left in the transferred wine to carry on the fermentation and continue breeding to produce more yeasts. The slow-down after racking does not last long.

It will be seen in my recipes that I advocate adding nutrients. These are blends of chemicals designed to stimulate yeast action and also help to balance the must. These also have the effect of shortening the period of fermentation but you should not add more than required. There are many nutrients and each supplier gives directions most suitable for those he supplies, so do stick to his directions. These usually amount to adding one tablet per gallon or perhaps a teaspoonful. Always crush the tablets beforehand.

Sweet or Dry?

As mentioned before, yeasts normally in every day use can produce up to 15 per cent of alcohol by volume, at which stage they are destroyed by the alcohol it has produced. Also mentioned is the fact that to produce this amount of alcohol in one gallon of wine approximately $2\frac{1}{2}$ pounds of sugar per gallon is required.

It will be seen from this that all sugar in addition to this $2\frac{1}{2}$ pounds will be left unfermented to sweeten. In the recipes, the amounts of sugar for sweet and dry are given. But those branching out on their own will find this information useful for it will allow them to adjust the sugar content to their needs.

Those making dry wines of less than 15 per cent of alcohol are advised to use the hydrometer which is described on page 52.

In the normal way, $2\frac{1}{2}$ pounds of sugar will make a dry wine of 15 per cent, 2 pounds 14 ounces will make a medium wine of the same strength. A sweet wine of the same alcohol content would require $3\frac{1}{4}$ pounds.

However, people's conception of dryness and sweetness varies considerably so that an ordinary dry wine is far too dry for them. Similarly, other people find that what one person calls a sweet wine is far too sweet for them.

The amounts of sugar in the recipes make the sweet or dry that suits the average palate. For this reason you may have to alter the amounts of sugar to meet your own special requirements. You will not be able to do this until you have made one or two batches so that you can decide whether they suit your palate or not. But be especially careful when making wines sweeter than I recommend because this fault is far more difficult to remedy than a dry wine that can always be sweetened.

Making lower alcohol dry wines is common practice today simply because they are better for being in the region of 10–11 per cent of alcohol rather than 15 per cent. Dry wines of 15 per cent have a harshness given into them by the amount of alcohol, whereas those of 10–11 per cent do not. In any case, dry wines are usually taken with meals where lower alcohol wines are preferred.

Do not imagine that wines of this strength are really low alcohol wines: many commercial products are as low as 9 per cent.

The higher percentage of alcohol is readily accepted in the sweeter wines. Indeed, it is required not only for itself but to act as a preservative, because sweet wines of lower alcohol content are liable to spoilage. On the other hand, lower alcohol dry wines are not so likely to be affected in this manner because there is no unfermented sugar left in the wine. And it is upon this sugar that many of the spoilage organisms begin their work.

As little as 2 pounds of sugar may be used to produce a very dry wine where the ingredients are suitable for this. If you see – as you will – in the recipes that a dry wine from any particular fruit is not recommended, do not be tempted to make it. This is because certain ingredients are better reserved for certain types of wines.

Choice of Yeast

Years ago we had only bakers' yeast or brewers' 'barm' to work with and while these made quite reasonable wines on occasions, they could not, and cannot today, hope to produce wines of the finer quality as made by wine yeasts, which are, after all, especially cultivated for the purpose.

Bakers' yeast has many drawbacks. It very often leaves a faint yeast cloud in the wine which is usually difficult to remove. Furthermore, it very often imparts a 'new bread' or bakehouse mustiness to the wines. And neither brewers' 'barm' (yeast) nor bakers' yeast are capable of withstanding so much alcohol as wine yeasts.

Wine yeasts, on the other hand, never leave a cloud in wine unless there is some other fault which holds it in suspension. This point is covered in the *Clarifying* sub-section. They are noted for their ability to settle to the bottom of the container and settle hard, so that they are not easily disturbed as bakers' yeast is. That yeast very often floats about loosely in the bottom inch or two of wine and is so easily disturbed that it rises up into clear wine at the least disturbance. But wine yeasts settle like firm jelly and stubbornly refuse to move unless the container is tipped at a steep angle.

This alone is a valuable asset but more important is that wine yeasts bring out the flavour of the fruits and produce much fuller wines with good bouquet and aroma. This is not to mention an all-important two or three per cent more alcohol.

And they are no more difficult to use than bakers' yeast but an important point to bear in mind here is that once having produced a must (prepared fruit juice and water mixture) it is of the utmost importance that fermentation is on the go as soon as possible. This is because even when we have sterilized a must, if it hangs about for two or three days without fermentation starting, there is risk of bacteria or wild yeast coming into contact with it even though it may be covered. But when fermentation is on the go the gas formed keeps up a constant outgoing stream through the puckers of the protective material. This prevents any troublesome organisms from gaining access.

For this reason it is wise to make what we call a nucleus

ferment: when we do this we add yeast already active. Bear in mind that all yeasts when purchased are dormant and must be activated before fermentation can begin, so by making a nucleus we are able to add already active yeast to our prepared mixtures so that the lot is in active fermentation within a few hours of it being added. Because of this it is a good plan to make the nucleus three days ahead of preparing the mixture to receive it.

Making a Nucleus

Any wine yeast may be made into a nucleus and most suppliers give directions for making one with their particular yeast.

Although I give independent directions here for use with any wine yeast, I would like to recommend to beginners the latest improved Respora yeasts which I have found excellent. This is not to say that other yeasts are not so good. It is just that this yeast – especially when used in conjunction with the nutrient known as Tronozymol – does give very excellent results. Most dealers listed at the end of this book stock these but if in difficulty they may be obtained direct from Fermenta, 58–60 Kingston Road, New Malden, Surrey. To make a nucleus, you merely boil about a quarter pint of water with a dessertspoonful of sugar and when this is cool put it into a half-pint bottle: then make this up to about half pint in a half-pint bottle with almost any sort of fruit juice, ie, orange juice, PLJ, concentrated grape juice or any sort you may have; even malt extract may be used.

To this add a little yeast, plug the neck with cotton wool and leave in the warm for a day or so; by this time it will be fermenting. When you have prepared your mixture for wine, shake the bottle, pour about half into the mixture and then make up the nucleus with a little more sugar, water and fruit juice so that you have another nucleus ready for the next batch. Although I have not found it essential to make a nucleus with Respora yeasts, it is always wise to do so just in case your must is slower than usual to get under way. Normally, this yeast is fermenting within a few hours but much depends on local conditions.

This yeast, like many others, is a general purpose yeast suitable for making all wines and it is with a general purpose yeast that most beginners will be interested. However, there are other more specialist types of yeast which are capable of giving varied results with different ingredients. For example, there are Burgundy yeast, Sherry yeast, Tokay yeast and so on. But these are not suitable for every sort of wine: they should be used with ingredients that make the sort of wine their names suggest. But do not be misled into thinking that a sherry yeast will make a wine flavoured of sherry: it will not.

One often reads of methods for making sherry together with sherry yeast and perhaps a sherry flor. But the method is not recommended because it means exposing the must to air over long periods and, as we have seen, this can cause trouble. Another point here is that the genuine sherry flor which grows on the surface of the wine is the secret of the sherry producers of Spain.

Another factor to be wary of is that over-exposure of the wine to air causes over-oxydation which is discussed under the heading of *Storing* on p 42.

Clarifying

As I have stressed elsewhere, nobody should have to use clarifiers simply because well-made wines will clear automatically. However, this is no help to those who, for some reason or other, fail to produce a wine that clarifies to brilliance in a week or two after fermentation has ceased and without assistance of any sort.

All the recipes in this book will make wines that will clear perfectly of their own accord. Those made by the sulphiting process cannot produce a cloudy wine provided a good yeast is used. But before I go any further, let me first explain the causes of cloudiness and say at the outset that cloudy wines are almost always the fault of the method.

There are, strictly speaking, only two types of cloudiness, one being caused by pectin and the other by starch. Cloudiness caused by pectin is produced when fruit juices are heated or boiled as was often recommended in old methods as a means of destroying the wild yeasts and bacteria that were present.

Pectin, which is found in all fruits in varying amounts, was boiled into the mixture and remained in suspension in the finished wine. Being a glutinous substance it not only remains in suspension itself but also holds other matter like minute fruit solids and the lighter particles of yeast to form a permanent cloudiness which only a pectin-destroying enzyme will remove.

Modern methods of destroying wild yeasts and bacteria with Campden tablets does away with the need to boil and therefore prevents the possibility of pectin causing trouble.

Ordinary clarifiers and even filtering will not make any difference to cloudiness caused by pectin or starch, no matter which filtering medium is used. Starch clouds – as they are called – are caused by starch holding minute solids in suspension in the same way as pectin. But this problem is encountered only with wines made with potatoes, parsnips, some other roots and sometimes apples.

The usual means of preventing a clouding problem when using these ingredients is to starve the yeast of sugar in the early stages of fermentation so that the yeast converts the starch to sugar and then ferments it out leaving a clear wine. In the usual way, this method is perfectly satisfactory; certainly, I never have a clearing problem when making wines with roots.

Starch-destroying enzymes are available but these are not suitable for adding at the start as is the pectin-destroying enzyme recommended in the chapter dealing in making wines from fruits by the heat treatment method. The best way to work is to follow the methods and if, by chance, a cloudy wine results, a starch-destroying enzyme may then be used as advised in the chapter on vegetable wines.

Roots, such as potatoes and parsnips, must be boiled in order to destroy soil bacteria. It is this boiling which brings the starch into the must so there is nothing we can do at the beginning to prevent this.

As already mentioned, the modern Campden method where Campden tablets are used to destroy wild yeast and bacteria on the fruits does away with the need to boil so there is no problem from pectin with this method.

But if readers want wines flavoured of semi-cooked or of a stewed fruit, as many do, boiling or heating to a certain degree is the only means of achieving this.

Up to a few years ago pectin-destroying enzymes were not available to us. Therefore, in order to obtain a clear wine we had to strain out every particle of pectin-bearing fruit and boil the juice only. This process had to be through a jelly bag which made it a lengthy though effective process.

Juices only do not give such good wines as those made when the fruit itself is fermented for a while but now that we have a cheap pectin-destroying enzyme ready to use we may boil or simmer the fruits themselves to obtain the cooked fruit flavour and at the same time be assured of a clear wine into the bargain.

Adding the enzyme known as Pectozyme is all part of the simple method of making these wines.

It will be seen that there are two methods for making fruit wines: 1, the Campden method for making wines flavoured of raw fruits and 2, the heat treatment method for those who prefer the cooked fruit flavour.

Sticking Ferments

This is the term used to describe a fermentation that has stopped before the maximum alcohol has been reached. This was the cause of wines fermenting again after they had been put away as finished products. Although this trouble is encountered today by inexperienced hobbyists on occasion, it is not nearly the problem it used to be.

When we had only bakers' yeast to work with and most people knew very little about the subject, when recipes were not balanced nearly so well as they are today, this was a common problem, so common in fact that it was the accepted thing to wait for what was thought to be a normal secondary fermentation to start up again in the spring. And this, of course, it did almost invariably.

Poor yeasts, lack of tannin or acid, or both, cold of early autumn, unnecessary interference and a general mishandling of the wines were (and still are where antiquated methods are still followed) the main causes of this problem, and what a problem it is (or should I say, was).

Either way, it is sometimes encountered today but this is rarely owing to the recipe or method because modern recipes and methods are balanced in order to produce top-class wines and at the same time put into the must the necessary constituents that the yeast needs if it is to ferment continuously until the maximum alcohol has been made.

This is the reason for adding acid and tannin where the ingredients lack these and this is the reason for using good yeasts and suitable nutrients. And, provided these are used, there should be no problems with sticking ferments.

Over-heating and too cold an atmosphere are the main causes of sticking ferment: so do make every effort to keep wines at a reasonably constant temperature of around 15 °C. (65 °F.).

If you find a wine has stopped before it should have done, try to ascertain the cause before taking any remedial action. Ask yourself if you have forgotten the acid or tannin or nutrient or if the temperature is too high or too low. If you can pinpoint the trouble yourself, do put it right but do not expect fermentation to start off right away. Stuck ferments are often difficult to get going again, so it may be a week or more before you see the bubbles rising again.

Additional nutrient is often helpful as is a new addition of yeast or a little of another batch of fermenting wine. These little tricks will often restart a sticking ferment, but again, do not expect it to start off right away.

A leaking bung with a fitted fermentation lock will often give the impression that fermentation has ceased before it should have done, especially during the later fermentation stages when bubbles are not easily seen owing to their scarcity or when the wine is in stone or plastic containers where the wine cannot be seen in any case.

If the gas escapes round the bung or where the fermentation lock enters the bung, there will not be enough pressure to move the solution in the lock; it will remain motionless in the 'u' bend, giving the impression that fermentation has stopped. If you are doubtful about the reliability of your cork bungs, run a little sealing or candle wax round where the bung enters the jar and where the lock enters the bung. Alternatively, use a rubber bung. These are readily obtainable with a hole to take the lock from suppliers of home winemaking equipment. Moisten them and they will slide in easily but they are often difficult to remove. So if you have one which takes a strong grip on the inside of the neck of the jar, ease it gently from all angles, turning the jar occasionally.

If you happen to find that a wine is fermenting again after having put it away as finished, merely fit a lock and bring it into the warm, leaving it until it has stopped again.

If the wine is bottled, find the rest of the batch, put it into a jar and fit a lock, leaving the wine in the warm until fermentation stops again.

Acid and Tannin

It will be seen that in certain recipes acid in the form of citric acid is advised with sometimes a little tartaric acid as well. It will also be seen that I recommend the addition of tea or grape tannin in certain recipes.

Both of these are important constituents not only of the must itself but of any finished wine. Without sufficient acid wines would lack bite or freshness and would on the whole be quite lifeless. Tea is a useful and convenient means of adding tannin. If you make a little strong tea and leave it standing too long you will, upon pouring a cup of tea with the customary milk and sugar, find that it has a harsh flavour. The harshness is caused by tannin and it is this harshness, but in a lesser degree, that we want in certain wines.

In the ordinary way, all English wild and garden fruits contain sufficient tannin and acid for our requirements. Indeed, some contain too much of either or both. Elderberries are a good example of a fruit containing too much tannin. For this reason it will be seen in my methods that the period of pulp fermentation is shorter in order to avoid too much tannin being given into the wine from the skins. This fruit is probably the only one we shall meet in all our winemaking that gives too much tannin into the wine. This is not really a fault if you are prepared to wait for two or three years before you drink your wine but most people are not prepared to wait that long, so the only thing to do is not to use too much of this ingredient and not to ferment it too long. Raspberries and rhubarb are good examples of fruits that contain too much acid. There are others, of course, but these two will do for examples.

In most cases an excess of tannin in the fruits themselves need not bother us simply because we will not be using the undiluted juice of English wild and garden fruits. In fact, it is for this very reason that we are unable to do so.

It is quite safe to say that the wines would be undrinkable if we used the undiluted juices of these fruits as we do grapes. This is because they are so acid from the winemaking point of view and so astringent that the wines made from them would be unpalatable. Agreed, we could alter this by using chemical apparatus and by balancing the acid content to obtain undiluted juice more in line with winemaking requirements but this is not for home operators. If it were, I would recommend it. As it is, only those with laboratory experience or perhaps a budding chemist would be able to handle the apparatus satisfactorily. In view of this we do the only sensible thing. We use so many pounds of fruit to the gallon and, in this way, we reduce constituents likely to spoil the wine to a point where they are no longer able to do so. In other words, we produce diluted fruit juice that will make a good wine with sufficient, but not too much, of any particular constituent.

It follows that provided the fruit is ripe the wine will be perfectly satisfactory.

So much for the acid and tannin in fruit. With roots (potatoes, parsnips, etc) and with grains such as wheat and, of course, flowers, we have no such problem simply because these ingredients contain neither acid nor tannin. Certain dried fruit can be classed in the same group although dried apricots and peaches contain a little acid.

It is for this reason that acid and tannin is recommended in recipes calling for these ingredients and, as mentioned, the simplest form (and the cheapest incidentally) is recommended. Citric acid costs about 5p for a two-oz packet. To obtain the equivalent in lemon juice you would need something like twenty good-sized lemons.

Oranges also contain citric acid and, where these are recommended, they not only add acid to the wine but also all important flavouring. This is not to say that wines in which orange juice is used will be flavoured of orange – they will not – but they add to the overall effect without the taste of orange being noticeable at all.

From this little discourse it will be seen that while winemaking is simple in itself, the evolution of recipes is not.

Good and reliable recipes are often the result of painstaking work spread over long periods to enable those evolving them to produce a recipe that will make a wine to suit the average palate. And that, of course, is all a recipe can do.

Clearly then, it may well be that when you are making wines you will realize that 'this one would be better still if there was a little more (or less) acid or perhaps a little more (or less) tannin'. Tastes vary to a far greater degree than most people imagine. Take, for example, people who like some of the very acid wines from the continent; other people would not look at them twice let alone drink them.

So it all boils down to learning as you go along how to produce the very wines that will be yours and yours only and this is quite a simple matter when you have a little experience.

However, this is not the only important consideration. These constituents are also needed in the must. It is for this reason that they are added at the start. Acid is of great assistance to the yeast in its quest to make the maximum alcohol. Indeed, a must lacking acid will ferment very slowly and is likely to fall foul to undesirable ferments not so much caused by the bacteria and wild yeast already mentioned but by lactic acid bacteria which give a sickly sweet taste (or should I say after-taste) to the wine.

Acid is essential then for a good and thorough fermentation which continues uninterrupted and ends quickly, having produced the maximum alcohol the yeast can make.

Tannin is also important as this assists the must to clear during fermentation and assists wines as soon as fermentation has ceased to clear rapidly.

All these points are taken care of in the recipes so now it is just a matter of following them carefully. Be that as it may, knowing what you are doing and why you are doing it is important, for it gives you the understanding necessary to break new ground of your own accord with confidence. And who knows, it may not be long before you are evolving recipes of your own and I jolly well hope you do.

Chapter 5

SIPHONING AND BOTTLING

There is no doubt that the final bottling of the finished product is a very joyous process but under no circumstances should you bottle wine just for the sake of it. Like most other winemakers I do like to have a nice stock of bottled wines nicely labelled and smartly sealed; however, this does not mean that I bottle my wines as soon as I can. I much prefer to leave them in jars for as long as possible, for it is while they are there that the many improvements take place that are discussed in the chapter on 'Maturing and Storing'.

Eventually however there will come the time when the wine has to be bottled and then you will need to use a siphon.

A siphon can be quite an elaborate affair or it can be a very simple one. In theory, all that is needed is a yard and a half of ordinary clear polythene tubing with a bore of about three-sixteenths of an inch. In practice, however, this tends to some extent to remain coiled so that it rarely reaches close to the bottom of the jar without a lot of manipulating: then quite suddenly it will dip down and suck up some of the deposit, thereby defeating the very purpose for which it is used. It is a good plan therefore to get a siphon tube from a dealer in winemaking equipment. These are made of glass and are about fifteen inches long with the last half inch of one end turned upwards. The polythene tube is attached to the other end. If this is a rather tighter fit than it should be, heat a couple of inches of the end of the tube in hot water so that it expands; it can then be slipped over the glass tube and as it cools it takes on a mighty grip.

The idea of the upturned end is to avoid sucking up the deposit. This end rests on the bottom of the jar but the up-

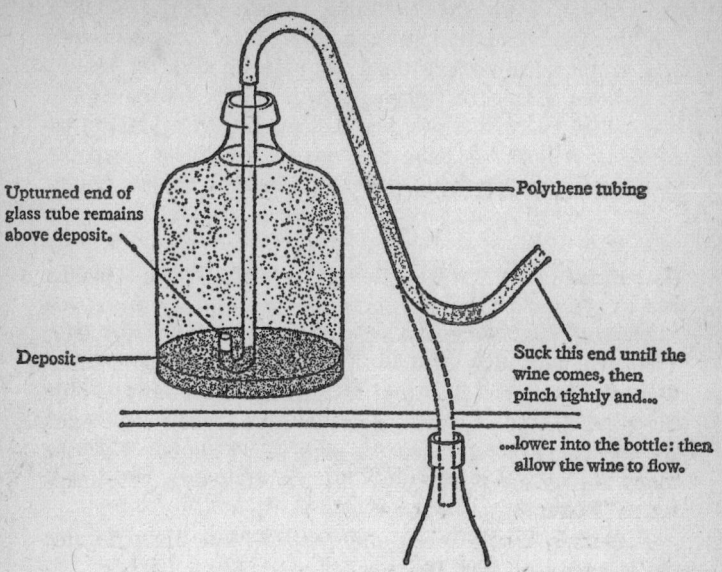

Upturned end of glass tube remains above deposit.

Polythene tubing

Deposit

Suck this end until the wine comes, then pinch tightly and...

...lower into the bottle: then allow the wine to flow.

turned opening remains above the deposit, so all you have to do is to arrange the full jars on a table and the bottles to receive the wine on the floor or on a stool. Bear in mind that the tops of the bottles must be lower than the bottom of the jar; if they are not, the last of the wine will not flow from the jar.

Insert the glass tube to the bottom of the jar and hold this firmly to avoid it moving about. Suck the end of the polythene tubing until the wine comes. Then pinch the tube tightly so as to hold up the flow. Put this end in the first bottle and let the wine flow. As the bottle fills watch for it to move into the neck of the bottle and pinch slowly so that as the wine reaches one-third of the way up the neck you can pinch the tube firmly to stop the flow while you transfer this end to the next bottle. If you are not careful to slow down the flow by gently pinching as the wine nears the neck of the bottle and have to pinch tightly and suddenly, there is a risk of the sudden halting of the flow churning up some of the deposit. Working in this manner you can empty a jar into six bottles in a couple of minutes without stopping the flow. If you do accidentally break the siphon (stop the flow), you have only to suck the end of the polythene tubing to start again. On no account fill bottles to more than one-third of the way up the neck. If you do, you should pour the excess into another bottle.

An important point to remember when bottling is that any wine accidentally spilled should be wiped up at once otherwise you can very easily attract undesirable organisms to this operation.

Corking the bottles should be carried out while the next bottle is being filled. Bear in mind that we do not want our wines to be exposed to the air for too long at this stage. This is not only because of the possibility of contamination by spoilage organisms, but also because of oxydation which is discussed in the chapter on 'Maturing and Storing'. Ordinarily wines at this stage contain sufficient alcohol to destroy any wild yeast and bacteria that may be lurking in the offing but the risk of over-exposure to air is there – so do not leave the wine uncorked for too long.

Having corked the bottles it is well worthwhile finishing them off with a decent label and a plastic seal. This gives your product that all important professional touch that your friends will admire. Years ago, one saw any old bottle, even cordial bottles, filled with wine with a cork sticking up half an inch or so and an irregular shaped piece of gummed paper for a label – and what a mouldy looking lot they were.

Today we are able to buy very cheaply colourful labels of many designs and also plastic seals like those found on various commercial products. These may be obtained by the gross from the suppliers or in smaller quantities from home-made wine supply firms. Whichever way you buy them bear in mind that those not being used must be kept in the solution in which they were supplied otherwise they will shrink and become useless. On average, they cost about a penny each.

All you have to do is to take one at a time, open it by twisting between finger and thumb, slip it over the top of the cork and press down all round, being careful to press out the little bubble that forms on the top and leave in an airy place to dry out. This it will do in an hour or so to effect a perfect airtight seal and complete the job of bottling.

Whether you use cork-made corks or the plastic sort, it is wise to use the flat-topped mushroom-shaped, otherwise known as flanged corks. These are easy to put in without a corking machine and just as easy to remove without a cork-screw. Wines bottled in this fashion may be stored upright; this is important for it sometimes happens, no matter how clear our wines may be, that after a year or so a slight deposit forms. If the bottles were stored on their sides this deposit would lie the length of the bottle and be tipped into the wine upon righting it.

When bottling, the choice of bottle is of the utmost importance. This is because dark red and even the paler red wines are often spoiled by light reaching them. A little light now and again such as when you open the door to your storage area will not matter but prolonged light will often take out almost all the colour and leave a wine quite flat to the palate.

If only for the sake of good appearance always use wine bottles and use dark glass for the reds and pale reds.

Lighter coloured wines such as those made from roots, certain dried fruits and flowers can be put into clear glass bottles. These always appear far more attractive if the bottle is of the punted variety: a punted bottle is one with the bottom pushed up inside.

The punt plays quite an important part for if by chance deposits form during storage, the punt prevents the deposit being disturbed until the very last of the wine is poured.

All wines may be stored in dark glass bottles if you wish.

Chapter 6

MATURING AND STORING

In effect, maturing and storing is one process and one which you have very little to do with. Nevertheless, it is a very important part of the process of making quality wines.

When finished wines are put into jars and bunged down as finished products, they are in reality far from finished. The changes which take place during this stage are just as important as the operations carried out earlier for it is only after this stage that the wine becomes a completely finished product.

To understand the maturing process fully is far from easy but we do know that chemical action and interactions are constantly taking place. Esters are formed and strengthening of flavour and bouquet takes place. This is not to say that these become more marked the longer the wine is stored because they do not. They reach their peak and are fixed – not lost – but held fast.

During this time oxygen is needed in the wine if desirable changes are to take place. Years ago in our efforts to protect our wines from the ravages of wine diseases we sealed them the moment we put them to store. This is not quite so necessary today because we are able to produce sufficient alcohol to preserve them.

When wine is stored in barrels oxygen percolates through the pores of the wood to bring about desirable oxydation and the professional vintner watches this process as he watches his bank account, for it is, of course, on this process that his bank account rests. When he is satisfied that sufficient oxydation has taken place he bottles his wine and seals it so that no further oxydation can take place. Over-oxydation causes wines to go flat and become quite lifeless.

I realize, of course, that keeping wines this long is not always possible because the hobbyist will want to use them but it is best to keep them if you possibly can.

As I have said elsewhere and on many occasions, no one is able to appreciate the vast improvements that take place unless they have experienced them and you cannot do this if you do not keep some of your wines long enough for them to become really top class.

Ordinarily, bone dry wines do not require more than six months in store unless they are a bit rough when put away but even then this roughness usually mellows down inside of six months. If you find a dry wine still on the harsh or rough side after six months then you should leave it a bit longer.

All my recipes are designed to produce a gallon of wine or thereabouts because it is with this that most beginners like to find their feet. It is a good plan to make two-gallon lots when you know what you are doing. In this way you can put one gallon away for a long time and use the other as required. In this way, you will have some to use and also be building up a useful stock at the same time.

Where to store is often a problem. I used to have a wonderfully cool dark cellar complete with a couple of spooks who used to help themselves to some of my best. At least so I thought until I found that my old Dad who taught me most of the ins and outs of this business also had a key. Cellars and those blessings, semi-basements, will soon be a thing of the past, so it's under the stairs for most of us. This is, normally, an ideal place.

However I am sure that the main consideration once wine has been put away is that it should not be disturbed so don't put it where you will have to put the vacuum cleaner or have to move it when the meter man calls.

Stone jars which do not admit light are best if your storage area is subject to strong light. Glass jars are suitable provided you can keep them in the dark. If you cannot, you should wrap them in dark brown paper or similar material which will exclude light.

I am not fond of the latest plastic storage containers as I

find that when used for a second or third time the wine appears to take on flavours that I cannot attribute to anything other than the plastic. Furthermore, they admit light and, contrary to most beliefs, they are not proof against strongly smelling substances.

I have not experienced this myself but a friend of mine who had an accident with a can of paraffin near his storage area found that a batch of wine in a plastic container had, very slightly, taken on the taste of paraffin. Alcohol tends to pick up flavours of this sort.

Because few amateurs store their wines in barrels it means that when wines are put into jars the only area through which oxygen can percolate is through the bung. So, when we put wine away with the bung rammed home tightly we must leave it like this for six months. This may not be long enough for all wines but we cannot keep taking samples to find out. After six months we can only presume that for most wines sufficient oxydation has taken place: then slice the bung off level with the top of the jar and cover the surface of the cork and rim of the jar with sealing wax or some other material that will effect airtight sealing.

Six months is likely to be enough for wines found to be smooth on putting away. Where the wine was found to be rough or harsh, nine months to a year would be better.

Having sealed the jar, it should remain undisturbed for at least another six months to a year. After this it may be bottled.

Those without suitable indoor storage space may use sheds or outhouses provided these do not become overheated during summer. A chap I know who has had central heating installed now stores his wine in the coal bunker. It is a bit deep but he seems not to mind: being of concrete slabs it is cool, dark and waterproof.

A similar but shallower arrangement would be easy to build with about three or four hundred bricks. If you embark upon anything of this sort do build on a concrete base, site it in a shaded area and use concrete slabs for the roof, which, of course, should overlap the walls to exclude rain seeping in.

This sort of building need be only a couple of inches deeper than the jars. Storage of wines in these modern days and in modern accommodation tends to present problems but it certainly is not deterring anybody from taking up the hobby, as is shown by the thousands who join us every month.

Bear in mind that there is nothing to compare with a stock of good wines, for not only does it mean that you always have a drink on hand for your own use but you can always open a bottle to entertain friends, even at the ungodly hours that some of them choose to turn up. Furthermore, a stock of decent wines is worth a lot of money.

Preserving and Fortifying

With present-day methods and recipes together with good yeasts and nutrients, we are assured of making wines with sufficient alcohol content to preserve them. Fourteen–fifteen per cent by volume is usually enough for this purpose and if all goes well we should achieve this without any trouble. That is, of course, provided we are using enough sugar to do so.

As already mentioned, it needs approximately two and a half pounds of sugar in one gallon of must to produce 15 per cent of alcohol by volume. The difference between alcohol by volume and per cent proof is shown in the appendix.

This two and a half pounds is not necessarily all added sugar because a little may be contained in the fruit. When following dry wine recipes you will not normally make 15 per cent by volume because you will not be adding enough sugar for this. Only where two and a half pounds or more are used will you make this amount. Therefore most dry wines will not contain 15 per cent but somewhere between 11 per cent and 14 per cent. At first sight it would appear that because the lower alcohol wines are not of sufficient alcohol strength to be preserved in their own right that we should add some sort of preservative. This is not, strictly speaking, absolutely necessary. On the whole, a well made dry wine will keep long enough for most people because they rarely keep them long, for the simple reason that they are ready to use so soon. If such wines were to be kept for several years then some sort of preservation might be advisable.

Having said that let me qualify the statement by adding that storage conditions and the manner of storage would count for a lot. Provided your storage area is cool and dark and that the bottles or other containers are sealed to make them perfectly airtight, there is no reason why dry wines should not keep well for several years. One proviso to this is that provided these wines are not carried from place to place at frequent intervals.

You have no doubt heard that certain types of wines will not travel and for this reason I mention in the chapter on storing that it is of great importance to keep the wine undisturbed. This is not only important for dry wines because all wines improve or are, at least, unspoiled by being left undisturbed. Sweet wines, as we have seen, should contain enough alcohol to preserve them and, provided they are airtight and in suitable storage conditions, they should also keep for years.

But this is of no help to those in doubt as to whether their wines will definitely keep or not, for we shall always have with us those winemakers beset by doubts and who have some sort of inferiority complex which convinces them that they could not possibly make wines that are all that good and that will keep and improve for years into the bargain.

For this reason the following notes on preserving are included.

Campden fruit-preserving tablets may be used for preserving wines with absolute safety and without tainting the wine or discolouring it in any way. What we do when using these is to use a very mild solution of the same material we use for sterilizing our musts and utensils.

Ordinarily one tablet is plenty for one gallon of wine but we may add two where the wine has a good flavour of its own. The approximate equivalent of eight tablets are allowed by law in commercial wines, so if we do use two, we are well within accepted limits.

Most commercial wines of less than 14 per cent of alcohol by volume are preserved in this manner so there is no reason at all for being shy of doing the same thing yourself. All you have to do is to crush the tablet to a fine powder with something non-metallic such as the bone handle of a knife or the end of a wooden spoon. Having done this take a little of the gallon to be preserved and mix in the powder thoroughly until it is all dissolved. If you use a fluid ounce measure or some other vessel where you can see through the bottom you will be able to tell. You may then add this to the bulk and stir it in or put it into an empty jar and fill up with the wine. I mention this because it is important that thorough dispersal takes place.

Wines preserved thus should still be sealed and stored in conditions already described. On no account try to treat one bottle at a time, though of course you can treat half a gallon by using half as many tablets.

Fortifying with added spirit which is another means of preserving is rather expensive, especially if carried out on a large scale. However, there will always be those hobbyists who want to make some special wines into something even better so let me mention the use of vodka. This spirit is ideal for the purpose because it is so readily available and has neither colour nor flavour to mar the colour or flavour of the wines.

As whisky and brandy always flavour wines they are added to, it is best to disregard them. One to two ounces of vodka to the ordinary wine bottle is plenty, bearing in mind that the standard British wine bottle holds 26 fluid ounces, when filled to the usual level. All British wines and many continental products are sold in these bottles but many continental wines come in bottles holding less.

If you want to be sure of the size of your bottles, keep a full-size whisky or gin bottle handy as a measure and fill this to the usual level. These also hold 26 fluid ounces and the contents of these should go into a standard British wine bottle. If it does not, you are not using standard British wine bottles.

I mention this because if you add 2 oz of vodka to smaller bottles you may be wasting this expensive stuff and making your wine a little stronger than you intended.

To achieve thorough mixing it is wise to put the spirit in

the bottle and fill up with wine. If you want to do the same with a gallon at a time, six to twelve ounces should be plenty: bear in mind that a half-bottle of vodka holds 13 oz.

Generally, I do not recommend preserving unless it is necessary and there is one simple test that can be carried out to prove whether any particular wine is stable or not. A stable wine will keep without being preserved for as long as you want to keep it. An unstable wine will often keep for a long time provided it is not exposed to air or disturbed unduly. However, since unstable wines tend to be unreliable, it is often best to preserve them either with spirit or Campden tablets.

The simple test is to put a small sample in a test tube or tiny bottle and to plug the neck with cotton wool. A similar sample from the same batch of wine is corked and sealed in another test tube.

Almost any chemist will let you have test tubes and suitable corks for about 2½p each.

Remember that these must be sterilized, rinsed thoroughly and dried before wine is put into them. The samples should be allowed to stand overnight in normal conditions but not in strong or direct light. To find whether this batch of wine is stable or not, examine them closely in good light. If both samples are the same colour, then the batch is stable. But if the sample plugged with cotton wool has turned a darker shade of the original colour or has altered its colour in any way, then this batch is not stable and preserving is advisable unless you propose to use it up within a few weeks.

Chapter 7

OVER-ACID WINES: HOW TO RECTIFY

Over-acidity in wines used to be such a common fault that most people put up with because they thought it was a characteristic of most home-made wines. This, of course, was nonsense. Over-acid wines are usually produced by using under-ripe fruits. As mentioned earlier, English wild and garden fruits are high in acid and when using recipes we dilute the juice in order to dilute the acid and, provided ripe fruits are used, the resulting wines will not be over-acid.

Some wines must be acid to the palate because they are designed to be so. But even these must not contain too much acid otherwise they become unpalatable.

Over-acidity can also be caused by using too much fruit. Many people think that the amount stated in a recipe is not really enough for a full-flavoured wine. Others (and there are still many of them) wrongly suppose that using more fruit produces more alcohol. This is one of the hangovers from Granny's day and is, along with a lot more stupid notions, gradually going the way all stupid notions should.

Today, we look for rather light-flavoured or delicately flavoured wines with a pleasing fruitiness and freshness rather than those lead-heavy soporific sorts likely to cause gout and irritability.

So we have the modern recipe with its smaller amount of fruit and, provided we follow the recipes and use ripe fruit, over-acid wines will not result.

But alas, not everybody ensures that fruits are ripe. They may appear ripe to the eye but this is often deceiving. For example, near-black blackberries or blackcurrants appear black. Yet two more days on the bushes would have made all the difference. A few semi-ripe fruits are not likely to do much harm but a fair proportion of the total amount being unripe certainly would.

If by accident you do happen to turn out an over-acid wine, do ensure that it is, in fact, over-acid. I make this point because very many young wines are rough and slightly acid to the palate and many people mistake this early roughness for over-acidity. Yet it is very often all part of a young wine that will eventually be lost with time.

Only after wine has been kept for a year are you really able to judge whether it is too acid or not. And if, after keeping for this long you find that you really must have less acid in it, only then is remedial action justified.

The simplest and often the most sensible means of adjusting the acid in a finished wine is to blend it with one that has not quite enough acid.

If this is done sensibly, the result can be quite sensational, because by reducing the acid in the one you automatically improve the other.

The golden rule when doing this is to use a fluid ounce measure and to have some small pieces of cheese on hand and several small glasses ready.

Put half a fluid ounce of the over-acid wine into a glass and add half a fluid ounce of another wine to this. Sample, and if all is well, you will know that one bottle of the acid wine will go well with one bottle of the other and you can then blend them in bulk. If it is not what you want, do not add to the sample but start again and add more of one or the other. Sample again, taking a little cheese beforehand in order to clear the palate so that the slight differences are easily detected. If you do this carefully, you will realize how easily wines can be changed.

All you have to do when you have the blend you want is to substitute bottles for half fluid ounces. So if you used half a fluid ounce of one with one fluid ounce of another you will know that one bottle of the one wine will go well with two bottles of the other sort.

When doing this sort of thing, always blend within the groups – fruit wines with fruit wines, root wines with root wines, etc. On no account blend root wines or flower wines or wines containing citrus fruits (oranges, etc) with red fruit wines. However, rhubarb wine may be blended with root wines and sometimes in small amounts with flower wines.

It is all a matter of common sense. All you have to do is to ask yourself – is this wine similar enough to that wine to be blended together or will the flavour of this contrast with or spoil the flavour of that one? Only you can decide in the light of what you have when the time comes.

It may happen that you accidentally turn out an over-acid wine and have nothing suitable to blend with it. If this happens, you may, after having kept it long enough to ensure that the acidity will not right itself, remove some of the acid by the following simple method.

Put a quart of the offending gallon into a glass or polythene jug. From this quart remove about half a pint. Into this half-pint stir about a quarter of an ounce of medicinal chalk (precipitated chalk) obtainable from the chemist. Having done this, stir the smaller sample into the larger one and leave covered until the chalk settles to the bottom and the wine becomes brilliant again. Then siphon the clear wine into the gallon. In this way you will remove the acid from one quart of the wine. In other words, you will have reduced the acid by one quarter.

What happens when you do this is that the acid in the quart is crystallized so that it settles to the bottom of the jug. The sample is therefore acid-free. Mix the acid-free sample well with the wine and you have, in effect, treated one gallon of wine.

I recommend siphoning the acid-free sample into the gallon, as opposed to pouring it, so that no chalk is allowed to enter the bulk. If this happened, there would be more acid removed than you want.

Having mixed the treated sample with the gallon, taste and, if all is well, that is all there is to be done. If the wine is still too acid, you may repeat the process using less chalk this time. Always bear in mind that undoctored wine is always best, so this treatment should only be regarded as a last resort.

Chapter 8

USING THE HYDROMETER

People who have been making wines for some time often ask me if the hydrometer is an essential part of winemaking equipment. I usually counter this by asking how long they have been making wines. It may be one year or it may be ten. Either way, if they have been making wines successfully without one, the question answers itself.

I am, and always will be, an advocate of simple straightforward methods and would be the last to try to persuade anyone to use anything that can be safely done without.

The hydrometer can be safely done without, yet it has its uses. And because this book is *The Complete Book of Home Winemaking*, details of its use must be included. Readers must decide for themselves whether to use it or not.

Let me begin by saying that the hydrometer cannot be used with any recipe in this book as it stands. This is because all of them produce less than one gallon of must at the outset. If you want to use the hydrometer with the recipes here, you will have to double all ingredients so that you start off with over one gallon.

Those working with their own recipes may do as they wish but it must be borne in mind that the hydrometer cannot be used with less than one gallon. This is because it is designed to tell us how much sugar the must contains per gallon. If there is only a gallon and a pint or if there is a gallon and three quarts or if you have as much as fifty gallons it does not matter. The hydrometer will tell you how much sugar is contained in each gallon. The fact that there is an odd pint or two over the gallon or gallons does not matter.

If for example you have a reading of 1·090 it means that

you have this amount of sugar in each gallon or part of a gallon.

The hydrometer is used with two main objectives in mind. One is in order to prevent too much sugar being added at the start.

As we have seen in other parts of this book, the yeast does not like too much sugar to start with; indeed, two pounds per gallon is usually near the limit. It will be seen that my recipes ensure against too much sugar added at the start. This is not to say that the yeast will not start fermenting in a must containing more than two pounds per gallon. It will and most likely it will ferment satisfactorily but it sometimes does not. For this reason, the hydrometer is used to ascertain the sugar content so that it can be adjusted if necessary. This is the reason you will see in all my methods that the sugar is added

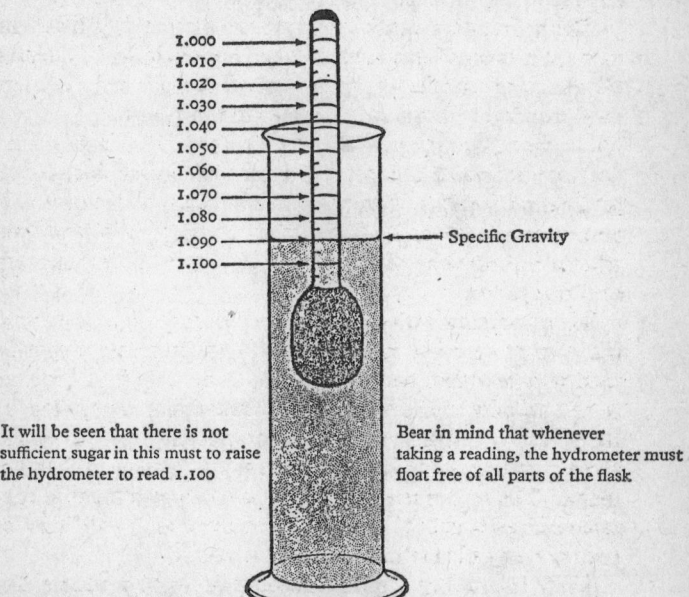

1.000
1.010
1.020
1.030
1.040
1.050
1.060
1.070
1.080
1.090 ——————→ Specific Gravity
1.100

It will be seen that there is not sufficient sugar in this must to raise the hydrometer to read 1.100

Bear in mind that whenever taking a reading, the hydrometer must float free of all parts of the flask

in two stages. And the fact remains that while a yeast will ferment in heavier concentrations of sugar, it will ferment more reliably in lower concentrations. So we have the modern methods which ensure against an excess of sugar in the must at any one time.

The second reason for using the hydrometer is so that you may ascertain with reasonable accuracy the amount of alcohol you have made. Many operators like to do this not only from the interest point of view but to help them decide whether to preserve their wines or not. If sufficient alcohol is produced, there is no need at all for either preserving or fortifying with spirit.

Generally, you will need two hydrometers; one reading from 1·000 to 1·100 and another reading from 1·100 to 1·200. There are many types of hydrometer now available for winemakers, some showing sugar content in pounds and ounces and at the same time showing the amount of alcohol to expect from a given amount of sugar but because in this business certain tables must run in opposite directions, the overall effect the beginner has when using this type of hydrometer is one of complete confusion.

So it is best to settle for the hydrometers mentioned so that everything is abundantly clear.

When using the hydrometer we take what we call the specific gravity of our musts. Specific means 'as compared with' and as we are using water as the specific, we are comparing our musts with water. Water has the gravity of 1·000; therefore, we compare our musts with that reading. If you float the hydrometer reading from 1·000 to 1·100 in sufficient water you will see that the water cuts across the stem at the reading 1·000 and this will clarify my meaning.

As mentioned, we use the hydrometer to find the sugar content of our musts. A must containing sugar will have a higher gravity than water. In other words, the must will be thicker, heavier or denser. These are not strictly accurate descriptions, but they do show what I mean.

In a must containing sugar the hydrometer will float higher than in water because of the density of the must owing to the sugar present. The height at which it floats depends on the amount of sugar present. Let us suppose that it floats at the reading shown in the illustration which is 1·090. It could be more or it could be less but this will do for the moment. This means that the must is denser or thicker to the extent of ·090 and this figure represents the amount of sugar in the must. Bear in mind that only the figure above the 1·000 is taken into account because the 1·000 is the gravity of water which we are using as a comparison. So we have specific gravity of 1·090. In other words, the sugar content of the must is ·090. If you now take a look at the hydrometer table you will see how much alcohol this amount of sugar will make.

If the reading shows that you have enough sugar to make the amount of alcohol you want, then all is well and nothing more need be done. On the other hand, if there is not sufficient sugar you will have to add some. Bear in mind that two and a quarter ounces of sugar registers 5 degrees on the hydrometer so for every five degrees you wish to raise the gravity by, you will have to add two and a quarter ounces of sugar. Because this is never added in its dry state owing to the problem of dissolving it, you have to turn the sugar into syrup by heating it in as little water as possible. A couple of tablespoonsful is usually enough for about 10 ounces. This amount of water is so small that it is not likely to affect the reading to any great extent.

When you have added the amount of sugar to give you the amount of alcohol you want to make, you should take the reading again to make sure you have added the right amount. If it is merely a degree or two out it will not matter all that much but if you must be precise, a little more sugar added as before will have to go in.

Bear in mind that you cannot make more alcohol than the yeast can make and that all sugar in excess of the amount that will make 15 per cent of alcohol by volume will remain unfermented.

It is best not to start with a gravity of ·100 (specific gravity 1·100) but it would be much simpler for beginners if they add the amount of sugar required to make the amount of alcohol they want and then later on when the gravity has dropped to about ·o6o (1·o6o) add the sugar needed to sweeten. This need only be about four or six ounces to the gallon.

The whole idea when taking the reading at the start and adjusting it as required is to find out the initial gravity – the gravity you are starting with. Then, when all fermentation has ceased, you take the reading again to find out how much sugar has been used up. In all cases the difference should be ·110 where more than this amount of sugar is used.

In other words, if you begin with a reading of 1·110, provided fermentation has been satisfactory, sugar representing ·110 degree on the hydrometer will have been used up, leaving you with a final reading of 1·000 or perhaps a fraction below this.

All that really has to be borne in mind is that provided fermentation is satisfactory, all the sugar in the must put there for the production of alcohol will be used up. But if you begin with a reading more (sugar) than ·110, say ·115, then you will end up with a reading of ·005 (specific gravity 1·005). As we have already seen that two and a quarter ounces of sugar registers 5° on the hydrometer, it will be seen that you have two and a quarter ounces of unfermented sugar left in the wine. The hydrometer table on page 57 will clarify my meaning.

Where dry wines are being made, the whole of the sugar will be used up, leaving you with a reading of 1·000 when all fermentation has ceased.

But if you begin with a specific gravity of 1·110 and then add sugar later on, as already suggested, several readings will have to be taken. Firstly, you will have to take the initial readings; then, when fermentation has used up some of the sugar, say after a week or ten days, you must take the reading again and record it. Sugar required to sweeten is then added, dissolved as already advised, and the new reading taken and recorded. When all fermentation has ceased, the final reading is taken and the total drop recorded. The effect of this is shown in the chart on page 58.

For example, if you begin with a reading of ·110 and after ten days have a reading of ·060, you will have had a drop of

·50. You then increase this by, say, 10 degrees, raising it to
·070. When all fermentation has ceased, the final reading is
taken and if all is well the reading should be 1·010. It will be
seen that you have had drops in reading of ·50 and ·60, which
makes a total drop of ·110.

It is just a matter of understanding that the more sugar
there is present, the higher the hydrometer will float. Con-
versely, as the sugar is used up by the yeast and less and less
is contained in the must, so the hydrometer will sink lower
and lower.

SPECIFIC GRAVITY TABLE

This table shows the drops in readings to expect when starting
with your desired specific gravity.

Specific Gravity	Gravity	Expected drop in readings	Sugar content at start approx	Sugar left unfermented
			lb oz	
1·120	·120	·110	2 13	10°–4½ oz
1·110	·110	·110	2 8½	nil
1·090	·090	·090	2 4	nil
1·080	·080	·080	2 –	nil

As you are unlikely to start with a lower specific gravity than
1·080, the table ends here.

SPECIFIC GRAVITY AND ALCOHOL TABLE

The table does not cover the full range as this is not necessary
but it does cover the range through which readers will pass.

Specific Gravity	Potential alcohol by volume per cent
1·080	10·5
1·090	11·9
1·100	13·4
1·110	14·5
1·120	16·0

Below will clarify what happens when sugar is added
during fermentation

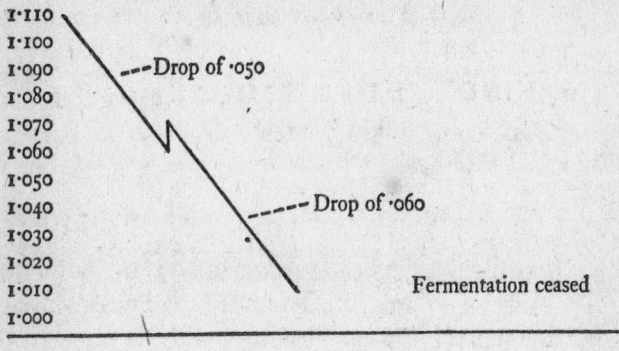

This shows that you began with a reading of 1·110. During
the process you increased gravity from ·060 to ·070. Drops
recorded total ·110.

Chapter 9

MAKING WINES BY THE CAMPDEN METHOD

This method is not only the simplest to put into operation but also the least troublesome. This is because we destroy all the trouble-causing wild yeasts and bacteria which are on the fruits (and about which I have already written) without applying heat in any way.

When we add the Campden solution to our prepared mixtures, wild yeasts and bacteria are destroyed by it. And as will be seen, we make up this Campden solution merely by crushing and dissolving a Campden fruit-preserving tablet in a little water. Now what could be simpler than that!

While this method is claimed to make wines flavoured of the raw fruit, this is not, strictly speaking, the truth. This is because many changes in flavour take place during fermentation so that blackberry or plum or damson wines do not necessarily have the flavours of those fruits when eaten raw. So let us settle this by saying that wines made by this method are not flavoured of semi-stewed fruits as is the case with many made by the heat treatment method. It is by the Campden method that we are able to imitate certain well-known commercial products while using wild and garden fruits. The Campden method has undoubtedly been the most popular for the past ten years or more and I am sure that it is with this method that beginners will want to find their feet.

When they have gained experience by working with this book, they will be able to deviate from my methods and recipes and work according to whim, using the knowledge gained as a basis from which to work. The heat treatment method for those who want to use it is described under that heading on p 89.

Avoidance of Repetition

In order to avoid too much repetition of directions in this, the Campden method, it will be seen that in the method for making the wines which appears after each recipe, the instructions read 'add the Campden solution' in the appropriate place. This is followed by the instruction 'cover as advised' also in the appropriate place. This has been done to spare readers the annoyance of too many identical instructions in each recipe or method.

Making the Campden Solution

Make this when it is required and not before. When you read 'add Campden solution', crush one Campden tablet to a powder and dissolve this in about an eggcupful of warm water and mix well into the pulp.

Cover as Advised

When you read this, cover the fermenting vessel with sheet polythene with no holes in it and tie it down tightly with thin strong string or hold in place with a strong elastic band. NOTE: I advise in all the methods to fill up the jar with boiled cooled water to where the neck begins. It nearly always happens that at the time this is advised, there is some space left in the jar. Much depends on how much sugar is used whether the space is large or small. Either way, the jar should be filled to where the neck begins as and when advised.

FRUIT WINES

Elderberry Wine

A full-bodied port-style.
3 lb elderberries, 3 fully ripe bananas, 3¼ lb sugar, yeast of

your choice, nutrient and approx 1 gallon of water as in method.

Strip elderberries from stalks, put them in fermenting vessel, crush well by hand and pour on half a gallon of water. Add Campden solution and leave covered while you boil half the sugar in 1 quart of water for two minutes. When this has cooled, mix well with the pulp. Then add yeast and nutrient, cover as advised and ferment for 7 days, stirring daily.

After three days, peel and pulp bananas and add this to the rest.

After seven days, strain and wring out tightly. Return strained wine to cleaned fermenting vessel. Boil remaining sugar in 1 pint of water for two minutes and when this has cooled, add to the rest. Cover as before and ferment for a further three to four days.

The next step is to pour carefully into a gallon jar leaving as much deposit behind as you can. If the jar is not filled up to where the neck begins, fill to this level with boiled cooled water. Fit a fermentation lock and leave until all fermentation has ceased.

Elderberry Wine

A lighter, fruity wine. Either medium dry, or medium sweet.

2½ lb elderberries, either 2¾ lb sugar or 3 lb, yeast of your choice, nutrient and approx 1 gallon of water as in method.

Strip elderberries from stalks and put them in fermenting vessel. Crush well by hand and pour on ½ gallon of water, mixing well. Add Campden solution. If making medium dry use the smaller amount of sugar. If making medium sweet use the larger amount. Boil half the sugar in 1 quart of water for two minutes and when it is cool mix well with the pulp. Add yeast and nutrient, cover as advised and ferment for five days, stirring daily.

After this, strain and wring out tightly. Return strained wine to cleaned fermenting vessel. Boil remaining sugar in 1 pint of water for two minutes and when cool, add to the rest.

Cover again as before and leave for a further three to four days. Then pour carefully into a gallon jar leaving as much deposit behind as you can. Fill up the jar with cooled boiled water to where the neck begins, fit a fermentation lock and leave until all fermentation has ceased.

Elderberry and Blackberry

A delightful Burgundy style.
1 lb elderberries, 2 lb blackberries, 3 lb sugar, 3 fully ripe bananas, yeast of your choice, nutrient and approx 1 gallon of water as in method.

Put berries in fermenting vessel and crush well by hand. Pour on ½ gallon of water and mix well. Add Campden solution.

Boil half the sugar in 1 quart of water for two minutes and when it is cool, mix with the pulp. Add yeast and nutrient, cover as advised and ferment for seven days, stirring daily.

After three days, peel and pulp bananas and add to the rest.

After seven days, strain and wring out tightly. Return strained wine to cleaned fermenting vessel. Boil remaining sugar in 1 pint of water for two minutes and when cool add to the rest. Leave covered as before for three to four days. Then pour carefully into a gallon jar leaving as much deposit behind as you can.

Having done this, fill up jar with cooled boiled water to where the neck begins, fit a fermentation lock and leave until all fermentation has ceased.

Elderberry and Raisin Wine

A full-bodied red wine.
2½ lb elderberries, 1 lb raisins, 2½ lb sugar, yeast of your choice, nutrient and approx 1 gallon of water as in method.

Put elderberries in fermenting vessel and crush well by hand. Add chopped raisins and then pour on ½ gallon of water and mix well. Add Campden solution.

Boil half the sugar in 1 quart of water for two minutes and

when it is cool, mix with the pulp. Add yeast and nutrient, cover as advised and ferment for seven days, stirring daily.

Strain and wring out tightly and return strained wine to cleaned fermenting vessel.

Boil remaining sugar in 1 pint of water for two minutes and, when it is cool, add to the rest.

Cover as before and leave for a further three to four days. Then pour carefully into a gallon jar leaving as much deposit behind as you can. Fill with cooled boiled water to where the neck begins, fit a fermentation lock and leave until all fermentation has ceased.

Another excellent wine may be made by using 1 lb elderberries with 1 lb blackberries and by following the above method. All other ingredients are the same as for the elderberry and raisin wine recipe.

Blackberry Wine

A good imitation of Beaujolais. Dry, of course.

2½ *lb blackberries, ½ lb sultanas, 2 lb sugar, yeast of your choice, nutrient and approx 1 gallon of water as in method.*

Put berries in fermenting vessel and crush well by hand. Add the chopped sultanas and pour on ½ gallon of water. Add Campden solution.

Boil all the sugar in 3 pints of water for two minutes and when it is cool, mix with the pulp.

Add yeast and nutrient, cover as advised and ferment for 8 days, stirring daily.

After this, strain, wring out as dry as you can and return strained wine to cleaned fermenting vessel. Leave covered as before for 3–4 days.

Pour carefully into a gallon jar leaving as much deposit behind as you can. Fill up jar with cooled boiled water to where the neck begins, fit a fermentation lock and leave until all fermentation has ceased.

Blackberry Wine

Burgundy style, sweeter than the above.
For medium sweet, use 3 lb sugar. For sweet, use 3½ lb. 4 lb blackberries, 4 fully ripe bananas, yeast of your choice, nutrient and approx 1 gallon of water as in method.

Put the berries in fermenting vessel and crush well by hand. Pour on ½ gallon of water, mix well and add the Campden solution.

Boil half the sugar in 1 quart of water for 2 minutes and when it is cool, stir into the pulp. Add yeast and nutrient, cover as advised and ferment for 10 days, stirring daily. After 6 days, peel and crush bananas and add pulp to the wine.

After 10 days, strain and wring out tightly. Return strained wine to cleaned fermenting vessel. Cover as before and leave for a further 3–4 days. After this, pour carefully into a gallon jar leaving as much deposit behind as you can. Fill up jar with cooled boiled water to where the neck begins, then fit a fermentation lock and leave until all fermentation has ceased.

Damson Wine

A delightful dry table wine, fresh and fruity.
4 lb damsons, 2¼ lb sugar, ½ lb sultanas, yeast of your choice, nutrient and approx 1 gallon of water as in method.

Remove stalks, put damsons in fermenting vessel and crush well by hand. Do not worry that this fruit gives little juice.

Add chopped sultanas and pour on ½ gallon of water and mix well. Add Campden solution.

Boil all the sugar in 3 pints of water for two minutes and when it is cool, mix into pulp. Cover as advised, and leave to ferment for 7 days, stirring daily.

Strain and wring out tightly and return strained wine to cleaned fermenting vessel. Cover as before and leave to ferment for further 3–4 days.

Then pour carefully into a gallon jar leaving as much deposit behind as you can. Fill up jar with cooled boiled water to where the neck begins and then fit a fermentation lock and leave until all fermentation has ceased.

Damson Wine

A heavy, full-bodied wine best kept for a year before use.
For medium sweet, use 2¼ lb sugar, for sweet use 2¾ lb. 6 lb damsons, 1 lb raisins, 4 fully ripe bananas, yeast of your choice, nutrient and approx 1 gallon of water as in method.

Put damsons in fermenting vessel and crush well by hand. Do not worry that this fruit gives little juice. Add chopped raisins, mix in ½ gallon of water and add the Campden solution.

Boil half the sugar in 1 quart of water for 2 minutes and, when it is cool, mix well into pulp. Add yeast and nutrient, cover as advised and ferment for 8 days, stirring daily.

After 4 days, peel bananas and pulp well and add this to the rest.

After 8 days, strain and wring out tightly. Return strained wine to cleaned fermenting vessel. Boil remaining sugar in 1 pint of water and add this to the rest. Cover as before and leave for a further 3–4 days.

Pour carefully into a gallon jar leaving as much deposit behind as you can. Fill up jar with cooled boiled water to where the neck begins, fit a fermentation lock and leave until all fermentation has ceased.

PLUM WINES

The following recipes are suitable for whichever plums you have, black, red or yellow, but do ensure that, whichever you use, they are fully ripe.

Naturally, each variety of plum gives different results but there is no need to vary the ingredients, so just use whichever plums you have. Yellow plums make for white wines while the others make differing shades of red.

All these wines improve vastly with age and should be kept

a year or two before use. The dry also improves but may be used much younger than this.

Plum Wine

A delightful dry type.

$3\frac{1}{2}$ *lb plums, $\frac{1}{2}$ lb sultanas, 2 lb sugar, yeast of your choice, nutrient and approx 1 gallon of water as in method.*

Put the plums in the fermenting vessel and crush well by hand. Add the chopped sultanas and mix in $\frac{1}{2}$ gallon of water. Add Campden solution.

Boil all the sugar in 3 pints of water for 2 minutes and when it is cool, mix into pulp. Add yeast and nutrient, cover as advised and ferment for 8 days, stirring daily.

The next step is to strain and wring out as dry as possible. Return strained wine to cleaned fermenting vessel and leave to ferment for a further 3–4 days, covered as before.

Pour carefully into a gallon jar leaving as much deposit behind as you can. Fill up the jar with cooled boiled water to where the neck begins, fit a fermentation lock and leave until all fermentation has ceased.

Plum and Elderberry Wine

A full-bodied, robust, but still a fruity wine that is not too heavy. Do not use yellow plums. Use $2\frac{1}{2}$ lb sugar for medium sweet or 3 lb for sweet.

4 lb plums, 1 lb elderberries, 1 lb raisins, 4 large fully ripe bananas, yeast of your choice, nutrient and approx 1 gallon of water as in method.

Put the plums and elderberries in fermenting vessel and crush well by hand. Add the chopped raisins and mix in $\frac{1}{2}$ gallon of water. Add Campden solution. Boil half the sugar in 1 quart of water for 2 minutes, and when it is cool, mix into pulp. Add yeast and nutrient, cover as advised and ferment for 8 days, stirring daily. After 4 days, peel bananas and pulp them and add this to the mixture.

After 8 days, strain out solids and wring out as dry as you

can. Return strained wine to cleaned fermenting vessel. Boil
remaining sugar in 1 pint of water for 2 minutes and when
cooled well, add to the rest. Cover as before and leave for a
further 3–4 days.

After this, pour carefully into a gallon jar leaving as much
deposit behind as you can. Then fill up the jar with cooled
boiled water to where the neck begins, fit a fermentation lock
and leave until all fermentation has ceased.

Plum and Raisin Wine

Another excellent full-bodied wine either medium sweet to
sweet may be made with plums and raisins. Follow the Plum
and Elderberry recipe and method in all details except for
leaving out the elderberries.

Plum and Blackberry Wine

A top-class wine of character. Follow the Plum and Elderberry recipe and method in every detail except to substitute
1½ lb blackberries for the 1 lb of elderberries. This may also
be medium sweet or sweet as required.

Green Gooseberry Wine

This one is, naturally, slightly on the acid side and should
be made thus and used as an appetizer. This is a fruit wine
with a pleasing freshness.

*2½ lb gooseberries, 2¼ lb sugar, yeast of your choice, nutrient
and approx 1 gallon of water as in method.*

Top and tail gooseberries, put them in the fermenting vessel
and crush well by hand. Mix in ½ gallon of water and add
Campden solution.

Boil all the sugar in 3 pints of water for 2 minutes and when
it is cool, mix into the pulp. Add yeast and nutrient, cover as
advised and leave to ferment for 7–8 days, stirring daily.

After this, strain and wring out tightly and return strained wine to cleaned fermenting vessel and leave covered as before for a further 3–4 days.

Then pour carefully into a gallon jar leaving as much deposit behind as you can. Fill up jar with cooled boiled water to where the neck begins and then fit a fermentation lock and leave until all fermentation has ceased.

Gooseberry and Sultana Wines

A little less acid, but fresh and fruity all the same and best made medium sweet. Gooseberries are not ideal for making sweet wines.

2 *lb gooseberries, 1 lb sultanas, 2¾ lb sugar, yeast of your choice, nutrient and approx 1 gallon of water as in method.*

Top and tail gooseberries, put them in fermenting vessel and crush well by hand. Add the chopped sultanas and mix in ½ gallon of water. Add Campden solution.

Boil half the sugar in 1 quart water for 2 minutes and when it is cool, mix into pulp. Add yeast and nutrient, cover as advised and leave to ferment for 8 days, stirring daily.

After this, strain and wring out tightly and return strained wine to cleaned fermenting vessel. Boil remaining sugar in 1 pint of water for 2 minutes. When cooled well, add to the rest. Cover as before and leave for a further 3–4 days.

Pour carefully into a gallon jar leaving as much deposit behind as you can. Fill up the jar with cooled boiled water to where the neck begins, fit a fermentation lock and leave until all fermentation has ceased.

BLACKCURRANT WINES

Several very excellent dry, medium or sweet wines may be made with this fruit. All of these have a delightful freshness and fruit flavour.

Blackcurrant Wine

A top-class dry.
2 lb blackcurrants, 2 lb sugar, yeast of your choice, nutrient and approx 1 gallon of water as in method.

Clean the fruit, place in fermenting vessel and crush well by hand. Pour on ½ gallon of water and mix this in and add the Campden solution.

Boil all the sugar in 3 pints of water for 2 minutes and when it is cool, mix into pulp. Add yeast and nutrient, cover as advised and ferment for 7 days, stirring daily.

After this, strain and wring out tightly and return strained wine to cleaned fermenting vessel. Cover as before and leave for a further 3–4 days.

The next step is to pour carefully into a gallon jar, leaving as much deposit behind as you can. Fill up the jar with cooled boiled water to where the neck begins, fit a fermentation lock and leave until all fermentation has ceased.

Blackcurrant and Sultana Wine

A full-bodied, medium sweet or sweet wine of character and distinction. For medium sweet, use 2½ lb sugar. For sweet, use 3 lb.
2½ lb blackcurrants, 1 lb sultanas, 4 fully ripe bananas, yeast of your choice, nutrient and approx 1 gallon of water as in method.

Put the currants in the fermenting vessel and crush well by hand. Add the chopped sultanas and pour on ½ gallon of water, mixing well. Add Campden solution. Boil half the sugar in 1 quart of water for 2 minutes and when it is cool, mix with the pulp. Add yeast and nutrient, cover as advised and leave to ferment for 10 days, stirring daily. After 6 days, peel and pulp bananas and add them to the rest.

After 10 days, strain and wring out tightly and return strained wine to cleaned fermenting vessel.

Boil remaining sugar in 1 pint of water for 2 minutes and when it is cool, add to the rest.

Cover as before and leave for a further 3–4 days. Pour carefully into a gallon jar leaving as much deposit behind as you can. Fill up the jar with cooled boiled water to where the neck begins, then fit a fermentation lock and leave until all fermentation has ceased.

Blackcurrant and Raisin Wine

If you have sufficient blackcurrants and can spare 4 pounds, this wine will be something quite out of the ordinary. Follow exactly the recipe and method for Blackcurrant and Sultana wine but substitute raisins for sultanas, use 4 lb blackcurrants instead of 2½ lb and use 3 lb of sugar.

You will need to keep this for two years for it to be at its best but what a beauty it will be.

RED AND WHITE CURRANT WINES

These two fruits used separately make for some very excellent light dry to medium sweet wines. They do not make sweet wines of good quality but the dry and medium sweet are fresh, fruity and all of delightful character.

The recipes specify redcurrants. If you haven't these, use white currants instead.

Redcurrant Wine

Dry.
2 lb redcurrants, 2 lb sugar, yeast of your choice, nutrient and approx 1 gallon of water as in method.

Put the currants in the fermenting vessel and crush well by hand. Pour on ½ gallon of water, mix this in and then add the Campden solution.

Boil all the sugar for 2 minutes in 3 pints of water and when it is cool, mix with the pulp. Add yeast and nutrient, cover as advised and leave to ferment for 8 days, stirring daily.

After 8 days, strain, wring out dry and pour carefully direct into a gallon jar leaving as much deposit behind as you can. Fill up jar with cooled boiled water to where the neck begins, fit a fermentation lock and leave until all fermentation has ceased.

Redcurrant Wine

Medium sweet.

2½ *lb redcurrants, 1 lb sultanas, 3 fully ripe bananas, 2½ lb sugar, yeast of your choice, nutrient and approx 1 gallon of water as in method.*

Put the currants in the fermenting vessel and crush well by hand. Add the chopped sultanas, pour on and mix in ½ gallon of water and then add the Campden solution.

Boil half the sugar in 1 quart of water for 2 minutes and when it is cool, mix with the pulp. Add yeast and nutrient, cover as advised and leave to ferment for 8 days, stirring daily. After 4 days, peel and pulp bananas and add them to the rest.

After this, strain and wring out tightly and return strained wine to cleaned fermenting vessel. Boil remaining sugar in 1 pint of water for 2 minutes and when cooled, add to the rest.

Cover again as before and leave to ferment for a further 3–4 days.

Pour carefully into a gallon jar leaving as much deposit behind as you can. Then fill up the jar with cooled boiled water to where the neck begins, fit a fermentation lock and leave until all fermentation has ceased.

SLOE WINE

This is a delight to experienced winemakers, but I must confess that I am not fond of it myself. Very often it is a matter of acquiring the taste for this wine, so you may well be disappointed. But a trial gallon is worthwhile making. Always best dry.

1 *lb sloes, 2¼ lb sugar, yeast of your choice, nutrient and approx 1 gallon of water.*

Put sloes in fermenting vessel and crush well by hand. Pour on and mix in ½ gallon of water and add the Campden solution.

Boil all the sugar in 3 pints of water for 2 minutes and, when it is cool, mix into pulp. Add yeast and nutrient, cover as advised and leave to ferment for 5 days only.

Strain and wring out tightly and pour directly into a gallon jar leaving as much deposit behind as you can.

After this, fill up with cooled boiled water to where the neck begins, fit a fermentation lock and leave until all fermentation has ceased.

PEACH WINES

On the whole, I have found that this fruit is best used for making dry to medium sweet wines. Very few people I have met like them sweet. Much astringency comes from the skins so peel three-quarters of them.

Peach Wine

Dry.

2½ *lb peaches, ½ lb sultanas, 2 lb sugar, yeast of your choice, nutrient and approx 1 gallon of water as in method.*

Halve the peaches and remove the stones, put the pieces in fermenting vessel and crush well by hand. Add chopped sultanas, mix in ½ gallon of water and add the Campden solution.

Boil all the sugar in 3 pints of water for 2 minutes and when it is cool, mix into pulp. Add yeast and nutrient, cover as advised and leave to ferment for 8 days. After this, strain and wring out tightly and pour directly into a gallon jar leaving as much deposit behind as you can. Then fill up the jar with cooled boiled water to where the neck begins, fit a fermentation lock and leave until all fermentation has ceased.

Peach Wine

Medium sweet.

3 *lb peaches, 1 lb sultanas, 3 fully ripe bananas, 2½ lb sugar, yeast of your choice, nutrient and approx 1 gallon of water as in method.*

Peel three-quarters of them, cut into halves and remove stones. Put the pieces in fermenting vessel and crush well by hand. Add chopped sultanas, mix in ½ gallon of water and add the Campden solution.

Boil half the sugar in 1 quart of water for 2 minutes and, when it is cool, mix into pulp. Add yeast and nutrient, cover as advised and leave to ferment for 10 days. After 6 days, peel bananas, pulp them and add this to the rest.

After 10 days, strain and wring out tightly and return strained wine to cleaned fermenting vessel. Boil remaining sugar in 1 pint of water for 2 minutes and, when it is cool, add to the rest.

Cover again as before and leave for a further 3–4 days. Then pour carefully into a gallon jar, leaving as much deposit behind as you can.

After this, fill up the jar with cooled boiled water to where the neck begins, fit a fermentation lock and leave until all fermentation has ceased.

Peach Wine

Sweet.

There is sure to be an odd reader here and there who must make this wine sweet – some people must have all wines sweet – so here are directions for those special readers.

Use the above recipe and method, but use a half-pound more peaches and a half-pound more sugar and peel only half the peaches before using them.

You will need to keep this one at least a year for it to be at its best.

It is very often possible on a Saturday evening to buy cheaply peaches that are fully ripe and which are likely to deteriorate if kept over the weekend. Have a word with your greengrocer or market stallman.

APRICOT WINES

Apricots have a slightly stronger flavour than peaches and for this reason a little less of them is needed for fully flavoured wines. Like peaches, I have found that these are best for making dry to medium sweet wines.

Apricot Wine

Dry.
2 lb apricots, 2¼ lb sugar, yeast of your choice, nutrient and approx 1 gallon of water as in method.

Halve the apricots and remove stones, put the halves in the fermenting vessel and crush well by hand. Mix in ½ gallon of water and add the Campden solution. Boil all the sugar in 1 quart of water for 2 minutes and when it is cool, mix into pulp. Add yeast and nutrient, cover as advised and ferment for ten days, stirring daily.

After this, strain and wring out tightly and let strained wine stand covered as before for about 2 hours. Then pour carefully into a gallon jar leaving as much deposit as you can. Fill up the jar with cooled boiled water to where the neck begins, fit a fermentation lock and leave until all fermentation has ceased.

Apricot Wine

Medium sweet.
2½ lb apricots, ½ lb raisins, 2¾ lb sugar, yeast of your choice, nutrient and approx 1 gallon of water as in method.

Halve the apricots and remove stones. Put halves into fermenting vessel and crush well by hand. Add chopped raisins, mix in ½ gallon of water and then add the Campden solution.

Boil half the sugar in 1 quart of water for 2 minutes and, when it is cool, mix into pulp. Add yeast and nutrient, cover as advised and leave to ferment for 10 days, stirring daily.

After this, strain and wring out tightly and return strained wine to cleaned fermenting vessel. Boil remaining sugar in 1

pint of water for 2 minutes and when cool add to the rest.

Cover again as before and leave for a further 3–4 days. Then pour carefully into a gallon jar leaving as much deposit behind as you can. Fill up the jar with cooled boiled water to where the neck begins, fit a fermentation lock and leave until all fermentation has ceased.

Apricot Wine

Sweet.

As mentioned, I am not in favour of making sweet wines with this fruit, but there are people who will want a sweet wine from them, so here goes. All you have to do is to follow the recipe for medium sweet apricot wine to the letter but using 3¼ lb of sugar instead of the 2¾ lb.

For those who want to make wines from nectarines, my advice is to make dry to medium sweet only and to follow the recipes and method for apricot wines but use half a pound more fruit in each case.

RHUBARB WINES

Years ago, rhubarb wines were something of a joke owing mainly to their weak flavour and over-acidity. Furthermore, they were often cloudy and were notorious for retaining the mustiness of bakers' yeast in their flavour.

Today it is a completely different story. They are popular not only as appetizer wines but also because by careful blending of ingredients one may make a variety of different wine types at very little cost.

This 'fruit' is plentiful and cheap and has a long season, so that anybody growing their own should be able to make a variety of wines at intervals from May to August.

Rhubarb Wine

Dry. A 'plain' wine, dry as a bone, with a pleasing acidity that is not too strong to the palate. Handled properly, this recipe could be claimed to make a delicately flavoured wine of character.

2 lb rhubarb, ½ lb sultanas, 2 lb sugar, ½ pint freshly made strong tea, yeast of your choice, nutrient and approx 1 gallon of water as in method.

Wipe the rhubarb clean with a damp cloth and cut into small chunks and crush with a rolling pin being careful not to lose any juice.

Put the pulp in fermenting vessel with chopped sultanas, mix in ½ gallon of water and add the Campden solution.

Boil all the sugar in 1 quart of water for 2 minutes and when cooled, add to the pulp. Add the tea, yeast and nutrient, cover as advised and leave to ferment for 8 days, stirring daily.

Strain and wring out tightly. Cover the strained wine as before and leave to stand for about an hour. Then pour carefully into a gallon jar leaving as much deposit behind as you can.

Having done this, fill up the jar with cooled boiled water to where the neck begins, fit a fermentation lock and leave until all fermentation has ceased.

Rhubarb Wine

Medium sweet. This makes a superb wine of character. It is fruity and fresh without being over-acid.

2½ lb rhubarb, 1 lb raisins, 2½ lb sugar, yeast of your choice, nutrient, ½ pint freshly made strong tea and approx 1 gallon of water as in method.

Wipe sticks clean with a damp cloth and cut into small chunks. Crush with a rolling pin being careful not to lose any juice. Put the pulp and juice in fermenting vessel with the chopped raisins, mix in ½ a gallon of water and add the Campden solution. Boil half the sugar in 1 quart of water for 2 minutes and, when it is cool, mix into pulp. Add yeast and nutrient and tea. Cover as advised and leave for 8 days, stirring daily.

After this, strain and wring out tightly and return strained wine to cleaned fermenting vessel. Boil remaining sugar in 1

pint of water for 2 minutes and, when it is cool, add to the rest. Cover as before and leave for a further 3–4 days.

After this, pour carefully into a gallon jar leaving as much deposit behind as you can. Then fill up the jar with cooled boiled water to where the neck begins, fit a fermentation lock and leave until all fermentation has ceased.

Rhubarb and Apple Wine

Another delightful dry wine, fruity and fresh. Use medium sweet or sweet apples of any variety.

1½ lb rhubarb, 1 lb apples, 1 lb raisins, 1½ lb sugar, 1 pint of freshly made strong tea, nutrient, yeast of your choice and approx 1 gallon water as in method.

Wipe rhubarb clean with a damp cloth, cut into small chunks and crush with a rolling pin, being careful not to lose any juice. Put the pulp in fermenting vessel.

Core and peel apples, chop finely without losing juice and put these with the rhubarb and add chopped raisins. Mix in ½ gallon of water and add the Campden solution.

Boil half the sugar in 1 quart of water for 2 minutes and, when it is cool, add it to the mixture. Add tea, yeast, nutrient and cover as advised. Leave to ferment for 10 days, stirring daily.

The next step is to strain and wring out tightly and return strained wine to cleaned fermenting vessel. Having done this, boil remaining sugar in 1 pint of water for 2 minutes and when cooled well, add to the rest. Cover as before and leave for a further 2–3 days.

After this, pour carefully into a gallon jar leaving as much deposit behind as you can. Then fill up the jar with cooled boiled water to where the neck begins, fit a fermentation lock and leave till all fermentation has ceased.

Someone is sure to want a sweet rhubarb wine although I do not consider it to be a good wine. Those who must have it sweet may use the above recipe and method to the letter but using 3 pounds of sugar. Those who want a medium sweet version may use 2½ pounds of sugar.

LOGANBERRY WINES

This fruit makes absolutely top-class wines whether made dry, medium or sweet. The wines may be made with quite small amounts of fruit.

Loganberry Wine

Dry. Fresh and not too fruity.
2 lb loganberries, 2 lb sugar, yeast of your choice, nutrient and approx 1 gallon of water as in method.

Hull loganberries and put them in fermenting vessel. Crush well by hand and mix in ½ gallon of water. Add Campden solution.

Boil all the sugar in 1 quart of water for 2 minutes and, when it is cool, mix with the pulp. Add yeast and nutrient, cover as advised and leave to ferment for 7 days, stirring daily.

After this, strain, wring out tightly. Leave strained wine, covered as before, for one hour. Then pour carefully into a gallon jar, leaving as much deposit behind as you can. Fill up the jar to where the neck begins with cooled boiled water, fit a fermentation lock and leave until all fermentation has ceased.

Loganberry Wine

Medium sweet.
2½ lb loganberries, ½ lb sultanas, 2¾ lb sugar, yeast of your choice, nutrient and approx 1 gallon of water as in method.

Hull loganberries, put them in fermenting vessel, crush well by hand and add the chopped sultanas. Mix in ½ gallon of water and add the Campden solution. Boil half the sugar in 1 quart of water for 2 minutes and, when it is cool, mix into the pulp. Add yeast and nutrient, cover as directed and ferment for 8 days, stirring daily.

After this, strain and wring out tightly and return strained wine to cleaned fermenting vessel. Boil remaining sugar in 1

pint of water for 2 minutes and, when it has cooled, add to the rest.

Cover again as before and leave for a further 3–4 days. Then pour carefully into a gallon jar leaving as much deposit behind as you can. Fill up the jar with cooled boiled water to where the neck begins, then fit a fermentation lock and leave until all fermentation has ceased.

Loganberry Wine

Sweet.

A sweet wine of character and distinction and one which will improve a good deal with age.

3 lb loganberries, 1 lb raisins, 3 fully ripe bananas, 3 lb sugar, yeast of your choice, nutrient and approx 1 gallon of water as in method.

Hull loganberries, put them in fermenting vessel, crush well by hand and add the chopped raisins. Mix in $\frac{1}{2}$ gallon of water and add Campden solution. Boil half the sugar in 1 quart of water for 2 minutes and, when it has cooled, mix into pulp. Add yeast and nutrient, cover as advised and leave to ferment for 10 days, stirring daily.

After 6 days, peel and pulp bananas and add pulp to the rest. Cover as before.

After 10 days, strain and wring out tightly. Return strained wine to cleaned fermenting vessel. Boil remaining sugar in 1 pint of water for 2 minutes and, when it is cool, add to the rest.

Cover as before and leave for a further 3–4 days.

Then pour carefully into a gallon jar leaving as much deposit behind as you can. Fill up the jar with cooled boiled water to where the neck begins, fit a fermentation lock and leave until all fermentation has ceased.

CHERRY WINES

Excellent when made dry to medium sweet but not at their best when sweet. Use black cherries.

Cherry Wine

Dry.
3 lb fully ripe cherries, ½ lb sultanas, 2 lb sugar, yeast of your choice, nutrient and approx 1 gallon of water as in method.

Remove stalks, put cherries in fermenting vessel and crush well by hand. Add chopped sultanas, mix in ½ gallon of water and add the Campden solution.

Boil all the sugar in 3 pints of water for 2 minutes and, when it has cooled, mix into the pulp. Add yeast and nutrient, cover as advised and leave to ferment for 8 days, stirring daily.

After this, strain and wring out tightly. Cover wine as before and leave to stand for an hour. Then pour carefully into a gallon jar leaving as much deposit behind as you can. Fill up the jar with cooled boiled water to where the neck begins, fit a fermentation lock and leave until all fermentation has ceased.

Cherry Wine

Medium dry.
3½ lb cherries, ½ lb sultanas, 2¾ lb sugar, yeast of your choice, nutrient and approx 1 gallon of water as in method.

Remove stalks, put cherries in fermenting vessel and crush well by hand. Add chopped sultanas, mix in ½ gallon of water and add Campden solution.

Boil half the sugar in 1 quart of water for 2 minutes and, when it has cooled, mix into the pulp. Add yeast and nutrient, cover as advised and leave to ferment for 10 days, stirring daily.

The next step is to strain and wring out tightly. Return strained wine to cleaned fermenting vessel. Boil remaining sugar in 1 pint of water for 2 minutes and, when it has cooled, add to the rest.

Cover as before and leave for a further 2–4 days. Then pour carefully into a gallon jar leaving as much deposit behind as you can. Fill up the jar with cooled boiled water to where the neck begins, fit a fermentation lock and leave until all fermentation has ceased.

STRAWBERRY WINE

Only suitable for making dry wines.

3 lb strawberries, 2 lb sugar, ¼ pint freshly made strong tea, yeast and nutrient and approx 1 gallon of water as in method.

Hull strawberries, put them in fermenting vessel and crush well by hand. Add tea and mix in ½ gallon of water and add Campden solution.

Boil all the sugar in 3 pints of water for 2 minutes and, when it has cooled, mix it into pulp. Add yeast and nutrient, cover as advised and leave to ferment for 7 days, stirring daily.

After this, strain and wring out tightly. Cover wine as before and leave to stand for one hour. Then pour carefully into a gallon jar leaving as much deposit behind as you can.

Fill up the jar with cooled boiled water to where the neck begins, fit a fermentation lock and leave until all fermentation has ceased.

ORANGE WINES

Three top-class wine types may be made with this fruit but you should be sure that you will like the flavour before you set out. Generally speaking wines made from oranges cannot be likened to any other wine type. This, of course, adds to their novelty. The medium sweet and sweet improve vastly upon keeping.

Orange Wine

Dry.

10 oranges, ½ lb raisins, 2 lb sugar, ¼ pint freshly made strong tea, yeast of your choice, nutrient and approx 1 gallon of water as in method.

Put the oranges in boiling water dunking each several times and then remove and dry with a coarse cloth. Quarter the oranges, put them in fermenting vessel and crush well by hand. Add chopped raisins and mix in ½ gallon of water and add the Campden solution.

Boil all the sugar in 3 pints of water for 2 minutes and, when it has cooled, mix it into pulp. Add yeast and nutrient, cover as advised and ferment for 10 days, stirring daily.

After 4 days, take the floating peel and press out the juice by hand as dry as you can and discard it. After 10 days, strain and wring out tightly. Cover wine as before and leave to stand for an hour. Add the tea.

After this, pour carefully into a gallon jar leaving as much deposit behind as you can. Fill up the jar with cooled boiled water to where the neck begins, fit a fermentation lock and leave until all fermentation has ceased.

Orange Wine

Medium dry.

12 *oranges, 1 lb raisins, ¼ pint freshly made strong tea, 2½ lb sugar, yeast of your choice, nutrient and approx 1 gallon of water as in method.*

Put the oranges in boiling water, pushing each under the surface several times and then remove and dry with a coarse cloth.

Quarter the oranges, put them in the fermenting vessel and crush well by hand. Add chopped raisins, mix in ½ gallon of water and add the Campden solution. Boil half the sugar in 1 quart of water for 2 minutes and, when it has cooled, add it to the mixture. Add yeast and nutrient and tea, cover as advised and leave to ferment for 10 days, stirring daily.

After 4 days, take the floating peel, press out as dry as you can by hand and discard it.

After 10 days, strain and wring out tightly and return strained wine to cleaned fermenting vessel. Boil remaining sugar in 1 pint of water for 2 minutes and, when cooled, add to the rest. Cover as before and leave for a further 3–4 days.

Then pour carefully into a gallon jar leaving as much deposit behind as you can. Fill up the jar with cooled boiled water to where the neck begins, fit a fermentation lock and leave until all fermentation has ceased.

Orange Wine

Sweet.
Use the recipe and method for orange wine medium dry except to use 14 oranges and 3 lb sugar.

RASPBERRY WINE

Difficult to make well. To be at its best it should always be light and dry.

1½ lb raspberries, ½ lb sultanas, 2¼ lb sugar, ¼ pint of freshly made strong tea, yeast of your choice, nutrient and approx 1 gallon of water as in method.

Hull raspberries, put them in fermenting vessel and crush well by hand. Add chopped sultanas, tea and Campden solution.

Boil all the sugar in 3 pints of water for 2 minutes and, when it has cooled, mix it into the pulp. Add yeast and nutrient, cover as advised and leave to ferment for 6 days.

Strain and wring out tightly. Leave strained wine to stand covered as before for an hour or so. Then pour carefully into a gallon jar leaving as much deposit behind as you can. Fill up the jar with cooled boiled water to where the neck begins, fit a fermentation lock and leave until all fermentation has ceased.

APPLE WINES

Some excellent wines resembling Sauternes may be made from apples. The main problem is producing the juice – apples being difficult to crush compared with other fruits. If it is intended to make large amounts, it would be wise to invest in a press or a fruit juicer. However, when making one-gallon lots, it is quite satisfactory either to slice the apples finely and then pulp them with the end of a rolling pin or just to grate them. If you grate them, use a plastic grater in order to avoid metal contamination. Prepare them only as required for use otherwise browning will take place.

Apple Wine

Dry. Use any variety, but preferably a mixture of two or three different sorts. This applies to all the recipes.

3 lb apples, ½ lb sultanas, 2 lb sugar, yeast of your choice, nutrient and approx 1 gallon of water as in method.

Peel and core the apples and prepare as mentioned above. Put them in fermenting vessel with about a quarter of the chopped peel and add the chopped sultanas. Mix in ½ gallon of water and add the Campden solution.

Boil all the sugar in 3 pints of water for two minutes and, when it has cooled, mix it into the pulp. Add yeast and nutrient, cover as advised and leave to ferment for 8–9 days, stirring daily.

After this, strain and wring out tightly and return strained wine to cleaned fermenting vessel. Cover again as before and leave for 2–3 more days.

Then pour carefully into a gallon jar leaving as much deposit behind as you can. Fill up the jar with cooled boiled water to where the neck begins, fit a fermentation lock and leave until all fermentation has ceased.

Apple Wine

Medium sweet.

4 lb apples, 1 lb raisins, 2½ lb sugar, yeast of your choice, nutrient and approx 1 gallon of water as in method.

Peel and core the apples and prepare as already mentioned. Put them in fermenting vessel with about a quarter of the chopped peel and add the chopped raisins. Mix in ½ gallon of water and add the Campden solution.

Boil half the sugar to be used in 1 quart of water for 2 minutes and, when it has cooled, mix it into the pulp. Add yeast and nutrient, cover as advised and leave to ferment for 8–9 days, stirring daily.

Then strain and wring out tightly and return strained wine to cleaned fermenting vessel. Boil remaining sugar in 1 pint of water for 2 minutes and, when it has cooled, add it to the rest.

Cover again as before and leave to ferment for a further 3–4 days. Then pour carefully into a gallon jar leaving as much deposit behind as you can. Fill up the jar with cooled boiled water to where the neck begins, fit a fermentation lock and leave until all fermentation has ceased.

Apple Wine

Sweet.
Follow the above recipe and method to the letter, but use 5 lb apples and 3 lb sugar. All other ingredients remain the same.

CRAB-APPLE WINES

Crab-apples make good dry to medium wines but are not really suitable for making into sweet ones. This fruit has an astringency found mainly in the skins but because the fruits are too small to peel, we use the whole fruits although rather less these days than in times gone by. Older recipes often recommend as much as a gallon of fruits to a gallon of wine. This is much too much by modern standards which demand rather more subtle flavours. Like apples, these will have to be grated through a polythene grater. Do not let any pips or parts of pips pass into the must.

Crab-apple Wine

Dry.
3 lb crab-apples, ½ lb raisins, 2¼ lb sugar, yeast of your choice, nutrient and approx 1 gallon of water as in method.

Grate the apples (see above) and put them in the fermenting vessel with the chopped raisins. Mix in ½ gallon of water and add the Campden solution.

Boil all the sugar in 3 pints of water for two minutes and, when it has cooled, mix it into pulp. Add yeast and nutrient, cover as advised and ferment for 8 days, stirring daily.

After this, strain out solids and wring out tightly. Leave the strained wine, covered as before, to stand for about an hour.

Then pour carefully into a gallon jar leaving as much deposit behind as you can. Then fill up the jar with cooled boiled water to where the neck begins, fit a fermentation lock and leave until all fermentation has ceased.

Crab-apple Wine

Medium.
4 lb crab-apples, 1 lb raisins, 2½ lb sugar, yeast of your choice, nutrient and approx 1 gallon water as in method.

Grate the apples (see notes above first recipe) and put them in the fermenting vessel with the chopped raisins. Mix in ½ gallon of water and add the Campden solution.

Boil half the sugar in 1 quart of water for 2 minutes and, when it has cooled, mix it into the pulp. Add yeast and nutrient, cover as advised and leave to ferment for 8 days, stirring daily.

Then strain and wring out tightly and return strained wine to cleaned fermenting vessel. Boil remaining sugar in 1 pint of water for 2 minutes and, when it has cooled, add it to the rest.

Cover as before and leave to ferment for a further 3–4 days. Then pour carefully into a gallon jar leaving as much deposit behind as you can. Fill up the jar with cooled boiled water to where the neck begins, fit a fermentation lock and leave until all fermentation has ceased.

PEAR WINES

Someone is sure to ask for a recipe for making pear wine, so I include these few notes. Pears alone do not in the normal way make good wines, and, in any case, they are best for making perry. Perry is a sparkling or fizzy wine – champagne style.

This type of wine is usually beyond the amateur, owing to

the process of producing the sparkle by natural means. This involves fermenting under screw stoppers, in itself reasonably easy, but too often results in exploding bottles which can also mean severe lacerations to anybody unfortunate enough to be in the vicinity at the time. Another problem is that if the champagne effect is obtained, there is always a yeast deposit that cannot be satisfactorily removed so that one almost always has a cloudy wine. Although the yeast settles down well as soon as the stopper is removed, the upsurge of captured gas always causes it to rise into the wine to cloud it. This type of wine *can* be made, as can sparkling beers which are far simpler, but I advise only those with years of experience to attempt to make them. Even these people will have to be skilled in the use of the hydrometer knowing how to allow for vagaries.

ROSÉ

Dry. This is an excellent wine and incidentally is the result of one of my most recent experiments.

Those who do not like bone dry wines should make this medium dry by using the larger amount of sugar listed. Do not make sweet.

½ *lb rhubarb, 1 lb blackcurrants, ½ lb raisins, 1¾ lb of sugar or 2½ lb sugar, yeast of your choice, nutrient and approx 1 gallon of water as in method.*

Remove stalks from blackcurrants. Wipe rhubarb clean with a damp cloth and cut into small chunks. Crush with a rolling pin being careful not to lose any juice. Put the pulp in fermenting vessel along with the blackcurrants and crush well together. Mix in ½ gallon of water and add the Campden solution.

Boil all the sugar in 3 pints of water for 2 minutes and, when it has cooled, mix it into the pulp. Add yeast and nutrient, cover as advised and leave to ferment for 9–10 days. After this, strain and wring out tightly. Cover wine as before and leave for about an hour.

Then pour carefully into a gallon jar leaving as much deposit behind as you can. Fill up the jar with cooled boiled water to where the neck begins, fit a fermentation lock and leave until all fermentation has ceased.

A similar vin rosé could be made by using blackberries instead of blackcurrants: any reader of an experimental turn of mind might like to try this. All that has to be done is to substitute 1 lb blackberries for the 1 lb blackcurrants: the recipe and method is otherwise followed to the letter.

Any reader may evolve recipes in this fashion merely by thinking to himself that 'surely if I can use such and such a fruit, a similar one would make a similar though different type of wine?'

Chapter 10

MAKING FRUIT WINES BY THE HEAT TREATMENT METHOD

This method, like the Campden method, has an enormous following and wines made by this method have distinctly different flavours from those made by the Campden method.

These flavours do, of course, resemble the fruits but are of the semi-cooked, stewed fruit variety.

As has already been explained, we must destroy wild yeasts and bacteria on the fruit. In this method we do this by heating the fruits instead of using Campden solution.

This heating alters the flavours of the fruits and at the same time releases pectin into the must: pectin, as we have seen, prevents wines from clearing. So what we have to do to obtain brilliantly clear wines when using this method is to use a pectin-destroying enzyme known as Pectozyme.

This is merely added at the time stated in the method; do not add sooner otherwise it may be destroyed by heat. Once destroyed it is, of course, useless.

Ordinarily half an ounce of the enzyme is enough for about five gallons of wine, so obviously very little Pectozyme is needed for one gallon. If making more than one gallon, increase the amount of Pectozyme proportionately as you would all other ingredients.

Avoidance of Repetition. In a book of this sort there is certain to be considerable unavoidable repetition, especially in the methods. To avoid too much, it will be seen that I recommend 'cover as advised'. When you read this, cover the fermenting vessel with sheet polythene with no holes in it and tie down tightly with thin strong string or hold firmly in place with a strong elastic band.

Bear in mind that not all fruits are suitable for this method, so use only those for which there are recipes. When heating the fruits themselves (not just pouring boiling water over them) use a saucepan of stainless steel, unchipped enamel, monel metal, or one with the latest non-stick interior.

The vessel used for boiling the water should not be of galvanized tin or chipped enamel. These are likely to give into the must minute particles of their metal. If this happens, fruit acids will attack them and give metallic flavours as well as displeasing colours into the wines.

BLACKBERRY WINES

A dry sort with a delicious fruitiness.

2 lb blackberries, 2 lb sugar, ½ lb raisins, juice of 1 lemon, yeast of your choice, nutrient, ½ teaspoonful Pectozyme and approx 1 gallon of water as in method.

Put the blackberries in a saucepan with 2 quarts of water and heat until just simmering. Put the chopped raisins and all the sugar in fermenting vessel and pour on the hot blackberries. Mix and stir well to dissolve the sugar.

Boil a further 3 pints of water and mix this into the pulp. When it has cooled, add the strained lemon juice and Pectozyme. Then add yeast and nutrient. Cover as advised and leave to ferment for 8 days, stirring daily.

After this, strain and wring out tightly and return strained wine to cleaned fermenting vessel. Cover as before and leave for a further 3–4 days. Then pour carefully into a gallon jar leaving as much deposit behind as you can.

Fill up the jar with cooled boiled water to where the neck begins, fit a fermentation lock and leave until all fermentation has ceased.

Blackberry Wine

Heavier, full-bodied, medium sweet to sweet.

3½ lb blackberries, 1 lb raisins, sugar: for medium, use 2¼ lb, for sweet, use 2¾ *lb,* ½ *teaspoonful Pectozyme, yeast of your choice, nutrient and approx* 1 *gallon of water as in method.*

Put the blackberries in 2 quarts of water and heat until just simmering. Put the chopped raisins and half the sugar in fermenting vessel and pour on the simmering blackberries, stirring until sugar is dissolved. Add a further 1 quart of boiling water and allow mixture to cool. Add yeast, nutrient and Pectozyme, cover as advised and leave to ferment for 8 days, stirring daily.

After this, strain and wring out tightly and return strained wine to cleaned fermenting vessel. Boil remaining sugar in 1 pint water for two minutes and when cooled, add to the rest.

Cover again as before and leave for a further 3–4 days. Then pour carefully into a gallon jar leaving as much deposit behind as you can. If necessary, fill up the jar with cooled boiled water to where the neck begins, fit a fermentation lock and leave until all fermentation has ceased.

Elderberry Wine

Rich ruby type, fully flavoured and quite full-bodied. Medium or sweet.

3 *lb elderberries,* 1 *lb raisins, sugar: for medium, use* 2½ *lb, for sweet, use* 3 *lb,* ½ *teaspoonful Pectozyme, yeast of your choice, nutrient and approx* 1 *gallon of water as in method.*

Put the elderberries in 5 pints of water, heat gently until it is nearly simmering and pour over the chopped raisins in fermenting vessel.

Boil half the sugar in 1 quart of water for two minutes and add to the rest while still boiling.

Allow mixture to cool and add yeast, nutrient and Pectozyme.

Cover as advised and allow to ferment for 5 days, stirring daily. After this, strain and wring out tightly and return strained wine to cleaned fermenting vessel.

Cover as before and leave for a further 3–4 days. Boil remaining sugar in 1 pint of water for two minutes and, when it has cooled, add to the rest. Leave for an hour and then pour carefully into gallon jar leaving as much deposit behind as you can.

If necessary, fill up the jar with cooled boiled water to where the neck begins, fit a fermentation lock and leave until all fermentation has ceased.

BLACKCURRANT WINES

As with the Campden method, three types may be made, all of which are top-class products.

Blackcurrant Wine

Dry.
2½ lb blackcurrants, 2 lb sugar, ½ teaspoonful Pectozyme, yeast of your choice, nutrient and approx 1 gallon of water as in method.

Put the blackcurrants in 3 quarts of water, and bring just to simmering and then pour into fermenting vessel. Boil all the sugar in 1 pint of water for two minutes and mix the two.

Allow mixture to cool thoroughly and add the Pectozyme, yeast and nutrient. Cover as advised and leave to ferment for 8 days, stirring daily.

After this, strain and wring out tightly and return strained wine to cleaned fermenting vessel. Cover as before and leave for a further 3–4 days. Then pour carefully into a gallon jar leaving as much deposit behind as you can.

If the jar is not filled to where the neck begins, fill to this level with cooled boiled water, then fit a fermentation lock and leave until all fermentation has ceased.

Blackcurrant Wine

Full-bodied, medium sweet or sweet.
3 lb blackcurrants, 1 lb raisins, 4 fully ripe bananas, 1 teaspoonful Pectozyme, yeast of your choice, sugar: for medium, use 2¼ lb, for sweet, use 2¾ lb, nutrient and approx 1 gallon of water as in method.

Put the blackcurrants in 3 quarts of water, bring just to simmering and pour onto the chopped raisins in the fermenting vessel. Boil half the sugar in 1 pint of water for two minutes and mix into pulp.

Allow mixture to cool thoroughly and add the Pectozyme, yeast and nutrient. Cover as advised and leave to ferment for 10 days stirring daily.

After this, strain and wring out tightly and return strained wine to cleaned fermenting vessel. Boil remaining sugar in ½ pint of water for two minutes and, when it has cooled, add it to the rest.

Skin and pulp bananas and boil these for two minutes in another ½ pint of water and, when it has cooled, mix it with the rest.

Cover as before and leave to ferment for a further 3–4 days. Then strain (several thicknesses of very fine material should be used this time and do not wring out) and allow wine to stand for one hour.

Then pour carefully into a gallon jar leaving as much deposit behind as you can. If the jar is not filled to where the neck begins, fill to this level with cooled boiled water, then fit a fermentation lock and leave until all fermentation has ceased.

DAMSON WINES

When using this method for damsons it is best to make the wines medium sweet to sweet. For medium sweet use the smaller amount of sugar and omit the bananas.

Damson Wine

4 lb damsons, 1 lb raisins, 4 fully ripe bananas, sugar: for medium, use 2½ lb, for sweet, use 3 lb, yeast of your choice, nutrient, 1 teaspoonful Pectozyme and water as in method.

Put the damsons in ½ gallon of water, boil until it is just simmering and pour while simmering over the chopped raisins in the fermenting vessel.

Boil half the sugar in 1 quart of water for two minutes and add to the rest while hot. Allow mixture to cool thoroughly and add the yeast, nutrient and Pectozyme. Cover as advised and leave to ferment for 8 days, stirring daily.

Boil remaining sugar in 1 pint of water and the pulped bananas in another pint, both for two minutes and, when they have cooled, mix them with the rest. Allow to ferment for a further 2–3 days.

Then strain and wring out tightly and return strained wine to cleaned fermenting vessel. Allow strained wine to stand for one hour and then pour carefully into a gallon jar leaving as much deposit behind as you can. If the jar is not filled to where the neck begins, fill to this level with cooled boiled water, then fit a fermentation lock and leave until all fermentation has ceased.

PLUM WINES

Red and black plums respond well to this method, but I have not found this the case with the yellow sorts.

Either red or black plums may be used in exactly the same way as damsons, so follow the above recipes and method to the letter using plums instead of damsons.

RHUBARB WINE

With this method I have found that rhubarb wines are best made medium sweet to sweet. Those liking the dry wine should use the Campden method.

3½ lb rhubarb, 1 lb raisins, sugar: for medium, use 2¼ lb, for sweet, use 2¾ lb, ½ teaspoonful Pectozyme, ¼ pint of tea, yeast, nutrient and water as in method.

Wipe the sticks clean with a damp cloth and cut into chunks. Put about half the rhubarb in 4 pints of water and heat until just simmering. Put the other half in the fermenting vessel with the chopped raisins and pour the simmering rhubarb over them.

Boil half the sugar in 3 pints of water for two minutes and, while boiling, pour over the rest.

Allow mixture to cool thoroughly, then add yeast, tea, nutrient and Pectozyme. Cover as advised and leave to ferment for 7 days, stirring daily.

Boil remaining sugar in 1 pint of water for 2 minutes and, when it has cooled, add to the rest. Leave covered as before for 3–4 days. Then strain, wring out tightly and return strained wine to cleaned fermenting vessel. Cover and leave for an hour and then pour carefully into a gallon jar leaving as much deposit behind as you can. Fill up the jar with cooled boiled water to where the neck begins, fit a fermentation lock and leave until all fermentation has ceased.

REDCURRANT WINE

Best made medium to sweet with this method. If you want dry use the Campden Method.

3 lb redcurrants, 1 lb sultanas, 1 teaspoonful Pectozyme, sugar: for medium, use 2¼ lb, for sweet, use 2¾ lb, yeast of your choice, nutrient and water as in method.

Put the redcurrants in ½ gallon of water and heat gently until nearly simmering. While hot pour over the chopped sultanas in the fermenting vessel.

Boil half the sugar in 3 pints of water for two minutes and pour while boiling into the mixture.

Allow mixture to cool thoroughly and then add yeast, nutrient and Pectozyme.

Cover as advised and leave to ferment for 8 days, stirring daily. After this, strain and wring out tightly and return strained wine to cleaned fermenting vessel.

Boil remaining sugar in 1 pint of water for 2 minutes and when cool add to the rest.

Cover as before and leave for a further 3–4 days. The next step is to pour carefully into a gallon jar leaving as much deposit behind as you can. Fill up the jar with cooled boiled water to where the neck begins, then fit a fermentation lock and leave until all fermentation has ceased.

BLACKBERRY AND ELDERBERRY

Excellent medium or sweet wine may be made by this method. These are deep red full-bodied and improve vastly with age.
2 lb blackberries, 1 lb elderberries, 1 lb raisins, 4 fully ripe bananas, 1 teaspoonful Pectozyme, yeast of your choice, nutrient, sugar: for medium, use 2¼ lb, for sweet, use 2¾ lb and water as in method.

Put the berries in ½ gallon of water and heat until just simmering. While simmering pour over the chopped raisins in the fermenting vessel. Boil half the sugar in 2 pints of water for 2 minutes and pour while boiling into the mixture.

Allow to cool thoroughly and add yeast, nutrient and Pectozyme. Cover as advised and leave to ferment for 7 days.

After this, strain and wring out tightly and return strained wine to cleaned fermenting vessel.

Boil remaining sugar in 1 pint of water and the pulped bananas in another pint both for 2 minutes. When both have cooled mix them into the rest. Cover as before and leave for a further 4–5 days. Then strain again, allow strained wine to stand for an hour and then pour carefully into a gallon jar leaving as much deposit behind as you can.

Fill up the jar with cooled boiled water to where the neck begins, then fit a fermentation lock and leave until all fermentation has ceased.

GOOSEBERRY WINE

Best made medium sweet only when using this method.
4 lb gooseberries, ½ lb sultanas, 2¾ lb sugar, ½ teaspoonful Pectozyme, yeast of your choice, nutrient and water as in method.

Put roughly half the gooseberries in ½ gallon of water and heat until simmering. Put the other half in fermenting vessel, crush well by hand and add the chopped sultanas. Pour the simmering gooseberries over the pulp.

Boil half the sugar in 3 pints of water for 2 minutes and

pour into mixture. When it has cooled thoroughly add the yeast, nutrient and Pectozyme. Cover as advised and ferment for 10 days, stirring daily.

The next step is to strain and wring out tightly and return strained wine to cleaned fermenting vessel. Cover as before and leave for a further 3–4 days. Then pour carefully into a gallon jar leaving as much deposit behind as you can.

Fill up the jar with cooled boiled water to where neck begins, fit a fermentation lock and leave until all fermentation has ceased.

RASPBERRY WINE

Does not make good sweet wine but when made medium sweet by this method this fruit makes a top-class product of its kind.

2½ *lb raspberries, ½ lb sultanas, 2 fully ripe bananas, 2¾ lb sugar, ½ teaspoonful Pectozyme, yeast of your choice, nutrient and water as in method.*

Put the raspberries in ½ gallon of water and heat until just simmering. While simmering pour over the chopped sultanas and pulped bananas in the fermenting vessel.

Boil half the sugar in 3 pints of water for 2 minutes and when cool add to the rest. When mixture has cooled thoroughly add the yeast, nutrient and Pectozyme. Cover as advised and ferment for 5 days, stirring daily.

After this, strain and wring out tightly and return strained wine to cleaned fermenting vessel. Boil remaining sugar in 1 pint of water for two minutes and, when it has cooled, add it to the rest. Cover again as before and leave for a further 5 days.

The next step is to pour carefully into a gallon jar leaving as much deposit behind as you can. If the jar is not filled to where the neck begins, fill to this level with cooled boiled water. Fit a fermentation lock and leave until all fermentation has ceased.

LOGANBERRY WINE

Top quality medium sweet to sweet wine may be made with this fruit and method. Both of these improve a great deal with age.

2½ lb loganberries, 1 lb sultanas, 1 teaspoonful Pectozyme, yeast of your choice, nutrient, sugar: for medium, use 2¼ lb, for sweet, use 2¾ lb and water as in method.

Chop the sultanas and put them in fermenting vessel with half the sugar. Put the loganberries in 3 pints of water and heat until just simmering. While hot pour over the sultanas.

At the same time as the loganberries are being treated boil a further 3 pints of water and pour over the pulp as soon as you can after the loganberries have been put into the vessel. Stir the mixture well to dissolve the sugar.

When it has cooled, add the Pectozyme, yeast and nutrient, cover as advised and leave to ferment for 8 days, stirring daily. After this, strain and wring out tightly and return strained wine to cleaned fermenting vessel. Boil remaining sugar in 1 pint of water for 2 minutes and, when it has cooled, add it to the rest. Cover again as before and leave for a further 3–4 days. Then pour carefully into a gallon jar leaving as much deposit behind as you can. Fill up the jar with cooled boiled water to where the neck begins if necessary, then fit a fermentation lock and leave until all fermentation has ceased.

Chapter 11

MAKING WINES FROM VEGETABLES

Wines made from vegetables are regarded by many people who use pre-packed, bottled and other high-speed ingredients, as hardly worth a second sniff let alone a second taste. This, of course, is snobbery for which there is absolutely no place in winemaking for the very simple reason that the whole secret of success in winemaking is making the wine you yourself like, regardless of the materials used. If an 'old sweat' happens to like wines made from Army boots and puttees, who has the right to question his tastes?

And so it is with all ingredients. I know of people who swear by their pea-pod or runner bean wine and politely disregard the mild ridicule of the ignorant. The fact is that roots and other garden materials make excellent wines of their type.

As mentioned in the chapter on clarifying, wines made with roots and perhaps other ingredients, as mentioned in this chapter, sometimes present a clearing problem. But with these recipes and methods brilliantly clear wines should result of their own accord. It is mainly where roots, potatoes, etc, are used that a clearing problem may arise. With these we cannot use a starch-destroying enzyme at the start as we use a pectin-destroying enzyme with fruits. Boiling in order to sterilize the roots and other ingredients causes the starch to be present in the must but if the method is handled properly, this starch should be converted to sugar by the yeast and fermented out, thereby leaving a perfectly clear wine. It will be seen that in some recipes I include the use of Pectozyme; this is because the ingredients contain pectin in the same way as fruits, but usually to a lesser degree.

The means of clarifying obstinate wines made from starch-bearing ingredients is described at the end of this chapter but I do not think you will have to use it – provided you are patient.

In the following recipes it will be seen that I recommend lemons and oranges and tea in certain proportions. This is done more for your convenience than for any other reason. Tea is a cheap and useful source of tannin but I do appreciate that lemons are expensive.

Therefore if you would rather use the cheaper citric acid from a chemist instead of lemons, bear in mind that approximately one ounce of this represents eight good-sized lemons. Where for example I recommend two lemons, a quarter ounce of citric acid may be used instead. Where the number of lemons is greater you may work it out for yourself. Usually a level teaspoonful of citric acid is sufficient but teaspoon sizes vary and for this reason it would be best to weigh out your requirement. Do not use extra citric acid instead of oranges.

If you would rather not use tea as recommended, a small saltspoonful of grape tannin may be used instead.

Potato Wine

Sweet or medium sweet. Use King Edward potatoes.
2 *lb potatoes, 1 lb raisins, 3 oranges, 3 lemons, 4 fully ripe bananas, ½ pint freshly made strong tea, sugar: for medium, use 2¼ lb, for sweet, use 2¾ lb, yeast, nutrient and water as in method.*

Chop the raisins and put them in fermenting vessel. Thoroughly scrub the potatoes, peel and discard the peel and cut up potatoes quite small. Put them in 5 pints of water and boil gently for 15 minutes: strain onto the raisins while simmering. Allow this mixture to cool and add the tea, strained juice of oranges and lemons, yeast and nutrient.

Cover as advised and leave to ferment for five days, stirring daily.

Then boil half the sugar in 2 pints of water for 2 minutes and, when it has cooled, add it to the rest. Cover as before and leave to ferment for a further 5 days, stirring daily.

After this, strain and wring out tightly and return strained wine to cleaned fermenting vessel. Boil remaining sugar in ½ pint of water and the pulped bananas in 1 pint of water, both for 2 minutes and, when it has cooled, add it to the wine. Cover again and leave for a further 5 days.

The next step is to strain again without letting too much deposit into the straining cloth. Then pour the strained wine into a gallon jar leaving as much deposit behind as you can.

If the jar is not filled to where the neck begins, fill to this level with cooled boiled water, then fit a fermentation lock and leave until all fermentation has ceased.

Parsnip Wine and Carrot Wine

Both these, like potato wines, are best made medium sweet or sweet and since the recipe and method for potato wines may be used for these ingredients, all you have to do is to follow that recipe and method to the letter except to substitute carrots or parsnips for potatoes and substitute sultanas for raisins.

Do not imagine that in doing this you will produce wines similar to the potato wines, for you will not. Indeed, they will be quite different and very good wines into the bargain.

Beetroot Wine

Excellent quality dry to medium wines may be made with beets. Not at their best when made sweet.

3 lb beetroots, 1 lb raisins, 3 lemons, ½ pint freshly made strong tea, sugar: for dry, use 1¾ lb, for medium, use 2¼ lb, yeast of your choice, nutrient and water as in method.

Clean and peel the beet thoroughly. Chop or cut small and put into 6 pints of water. Bring to boil and simmer gently for 15 minutes.

Put the chopped raisins in fermenting vessel with half the sugar and strain the simmering beets over them and discard the beet after allowing to drain.

When the mixture has cooled add the strained lemon juice, tea, yeast and nutrient. Cover as advised and leave to ferment for 8 days, stirring daily.

The next step is to strain and wring out tightly and return strained wine to cleaned fermenting vessel. Boil remaining sugar in 2 pints of water for two minutes and, when it has cooled, add it to the rest.

Again cover as before and leave for a further 3–4 days. Then pour carefully into a gallon jar, leaving as much deposit behind as you can. If the jar is not filled to where the neck begins, fill to this level with cooled boiled water. Fit a fermentation lock and leave until all fermentation has ceased.

Pea Pod Wine

Excellent dry to medium dry light wines are made with pea pods. The pods should have any blemishes or bad patches cut out. On no account allow peas into the mixture – not even the tiniest one.

3 lb pea pods, ½ lb sultanas, 3 lemons, ½ pint freshly made strong tea, yeast of your choice, nutrient, sugar: for dry, use 1¾ lb, for medium, use 2½ lb, water as in method, ½ teaspoonful Pectozyme.

Wash the pods thoroughly, put them in 7 pints of water and bring to boil and simmer until tender.

Put all the sugar with the chopped sultanas in the fermenting vessel and strain simmering pea pods onto them. Discard the pods and stir until sugar is dissolved.

When the mixture has cooled, add the tea, strained lemon juice and Pectozyme. Then add yeast and nutrient. Cover as advised and leave to ferment for 8–9 days, stirring daily.

Then strain and wring out tightly and return strained wine to cleaned fermenting vessel. Cover as before after this, and leave for a further 3–4 days. Then pour carefully into a gallon jar leaving as much deposit behind as you can.

Fill up the jar with cooled boiled water to where the neck begins, then fit a fermentation lock and leave until all fermentation has ceased.

Runner Bean Wine

Like pea pods, these make light dry or medium dry wines of excellent quality.

3 *lb runner beans,* ½ *lb raisins,* 2 *lemons,* 2 *oranges,* ½ *pint freshly made strong tea, yeast of your choice, nutrient,* ⅓ *teaspoonful Pectozyme, sugar: for dry, use* 1¾ *lb, for medium, use* 2½ *lb and water as in method.*

Wash the beans and prepare as for cooking removing the little pieces of beans. Put them in 7 pints of water, bring to boil and simmer gently until tender.

Put all the sugar with the chopped raisins in the fermenting vessel and strain the simmering beans over them, press out the juice and discard the beans. Stir mixture until sugar is dissolved.

When the mixture has cooled, add the tea, yeast, nutrient, Pectozyme and strained juice of oranges and lemons. Cover as advised and leave to ferment for 8–9 days, stirring daily.

After this, strain and wring out tightly and return strained wine to cleaned fermenting vessel. Cover as before and leave for a further 3–4 days.

Then pour carefully into a gallon jar leaving as much deposit behind as you can. Fill up the jar with cooled boiled water to where the neck begins, fit a fermentation lock and leave until all fermentation has ceased.

Parsley Wine

A delightful wine, golden light dry, or medium.

½ *lb parsley,* 1 *lb raisins,* 3 *lemons,* ½ *pint freshly made strong tea, yeast of your choice, nutrient, sugar: for dry, use* 1¾ *lb, for medium, use* 2¼ *lb and water as in method.*

Thoroughly wash parsley and bring to boil in 7 pints of water and simmer gently for 15 minutes together with the grated rinds of the lemons.

Put the chopped raisins and all the sugar in fermenting vessel and strain the parsley over them. Press well and discard the parsley. Stir until sugar is dissolved. When the mixture has cooled add the tea, strained juice of lemons, yeast and nutrient. Cover as advised and leave to ferment for 8 days, stirring daily.

After this, strain and wring out tightly and return strained wine to cleaned fermenting vessel. Leave covered as before for 3–4 days.

Then pour carefully into a gallon jar leaving as much deposit behind as you can. Fill up the jar with cooled boiled water to where the neck begins, fit a fermentation lock and leave until all fermentation has ceased.

Clearing Starch Cloud

As already mentioned there should be no need to resort to the two following methods of clarifying wines made with starch-bearing ingredients. If you have followed the methods carefully, the wines should become brilliant in a few weeks – especially if kept in the cold. If the weather is warm when the wines finish fermenting, put them away and forget about them until the cold of winter. Don't be afraid to stand them where they will become very cold – even a shed or outhouse that gets frozen out will not harm them and is very likely to clear them in a very short time.

I have mentioned earlier that only a starch-destroying enzyme will remove starch clouds. Certainly, filtering and the more usual clarifiers such as white of egg, isinglass and gelatine will have no effect at all – except to worsen matters in certain cases.

However, if cold fails to clear obstinate wines of starch cloud, there is one clarifier you might try before resorting to the rather troublesome method of using the starch-destroying enzyme known as Amylozine 100.

This is known as Pectasin. About one-eighth of a teaspoonful is mixed thoroughly with a little of the wine and then stirred into the bulk. The amount mentioned is usually enough for up to two gallons, and you may expect perfect clarity to result in a day or so.

If everything else fails to clear starch from a certain batch and it is really too cloudy to be palatable, then resorting to the use of a starch-destroying enzyme is justified provided the amount to be treated is a worthwhile amount for the trouble involved.

Take half an ounce of Amylozyme 100 and stir this into 3 fluid ounces of the wine to be treated. Allow the sample to stand for an hour or so with occasional stirring. Heat the bulk of the wine to 75°C. (170°F.) and keep at that temperature for 20 minutes. Then let it cool to 40° C. (110° F.). At this stage the enzyme may be added to the bulk and the treated wine kept in a cool place for a few hours – by which time perfect clarifying will have taken place. After this the clear wine is siphoned off the deposit.

Chapter 12

MAKING WINES FROM DRIED FRUITS

Those without gardens or not within easy reach of wild fruits will find these recipes a real blessing.

Making wines from dried fruits has become very popular in recent years because they are so readily obtainable in shops. Being wrapped in polythene or otherwise packeted it means that they are clean, much fresher than in days gone by and, very often, in a sterile condition.

But we cannot be sure of this, so scald them we must, to be on the safe side.

In the normal way, wines made with dried fruit never produce a clearing problem. However, it does seem that some people are prone to troubles that others never meet up with so I include in these recipes the use of Pectozyme just to be on the safe side. The use of this enzyme has been described in the chapter on 'Making Fruit Wines by the Heat Treatment Method'.

Dried fruit usually contains no acid and no tannin. When it does, they are in such small amounts that their presence may be disregarded. For this reason we must add both if we are to obtain a balanced wine of quality. In the recipes acid is recommended in the form of lemon juice and tannin in the form of tea. If you want to use grape tannin and citric acid instead of these, the proportionate quantities are given in the chapter on root wines.

Imported dried fruits: raisins, sultanas, etc, contain approximately 50 per cent sugar, so it will be seen that in these recipes very little sugar is required. But English dried fruit, such as elderberries and bilberries, contain so little that the normal amount of sugar for the type of wine being made is required.

Elderberries and bilberries are, I consider, unnecessarily expensive, so try several dealers in home winemaking ingredients before you buy. Bear in mind though that so very little of the English wild fruits are needed for one gallon that the wine is not necessarily expensive.

Dried fruit wines are, of course, excellent. If they were not, I would not be offering you recipes, for I never include in any of my books recipes that will not make top-class wines of their type.

An oddity I think you will experience with wines made from imported dried fruit is that the sediment or deposit is always thicker than with other fruits.

This is no problem, because racking from the fermenting vessel to the jar rids the wine of most of it and after this stage only a very small amount of fruit particles remain to settle out along with the usual yeast deposit that builds up in the jar. However, I decided to mention this in case one or two of you become puzzled or, worse, alarmed and therefore imagine something to be wrong.

Cover as Advised. As has been mentioned it is most important to cover the fermenting wine. But to avoid having to write out fully the same direction in each recipe, when you read 'cover as advised' cover the vessel with sheet polythene with no holes in it and tie this down tightly with thin strong string or hold it in place with a strong elastic band.

Fill Jar to where Neck Begins. This is another repeated instruction, but it is not always necessary to do this. But if there is any space left when all the wine is put into the jar, fill the jar up with cooled boiled water to where the neck begins.

Dried Prune Wine

Dried prunes make excellent medium to sweet wines that improve a great deal with age. They become full-bodied and quite robust.

For medium. 2 lb prunes, 2½ lb sugar, 3 lemons, ¼ pint strong tea, ½ teaspoonful Pectozyme, yeast of your choice, nutrient and approx 1 gallon of water as in method.

For sweet. 3 lb prunes, 2½ lb sugar, 4 lemons, ½ teaspoonful Pectozyme, ¼ pint freshly made strong tea, yeast of your choice, nutrient and approx 1 gallon of water as in method.

Put the prunes in 7 pints of water and leave to soak until swollen. Then bring to boil and simmer gently with the lid on until tender.

Pour the simmering prunes over half the sugar in fermenting vessel and stir well to dissolve the sugar. When cooled, crush the prunes and add the tea, strained lemon juice, Pectozyme, yeast and nutrient. Cover as advised and leave to ferment for 7 days.

Then strain and wring out as dry as you can and return strained wine to cleaned fermenting vessel.

Boil remaining sugar in 1 pint of water for 2 minutes and when cooled add to the rest.

Cover as before and leave for a further 4–5 days. Then pour carefully into a gallon jar leaving as much deposit behind as you can. Then fill up the jar with cooled boiled water to where the neck begins, fit a fermentation lock and leave until all fermentation has ceased.

Raisin Wine

When raisins are used as the basic ingredient they are best used for making a medium wine. Raisins are, strictly speaking, best used as an adjunct of other ingredients which they often improve. As medium sweet, the wine is excellent.

3 lb raisins, 3 lemons, 3 oranges, ¼ pint strong tea, ½ teaspoonful Pectozyme, yeast of your choice, nutrient and approx 1 gallon of water as in method, and 1½ lb sugar.

Chop finely or mince the raisins and put them in fermenting vessel with half the sugar. Pour on 7 pints of boiling water and stir well to dissolve the sugar.

Grate the lemon rind and orange peel over the raisins and

when the mixture is cool, add the strained orange and lemon juice. Add the tea, Pectozyme, yeast and nutrient, cover as advised and leave to ferment for 9 days, stirring daily.

After this, strain and wring out tightly and return strained wine to cleaned fermenting vessel. Boil remaining sugar in ½ pint of water for 2 minutes and, when it has cooled, add it to the rest. Cover as before and leave for a further 3–4 days.

Then pour carefully into a gallon jar leaving as much deposit behind as you can. Having done this, fill up the jar with cooled boiled water to where the neck begins, fit a fermentation lock and leave until all fermentation has ceased.

Sultana Wine

Two excellent wines may be made with sultanas when used with grapefruits. The sultanas give the background to the wine while the grapefruits put on what we might call an excellent front. The combined effect is a light refreshing wine when dry: when medium it is not unlike hock.

3 lb sultanas, 2 grapefruits (these provide the necessary acid), ¼ pint strong tea, ½ teaspoonful Pectozyme, yeast of your choice, nutrient, sugar: for dry, use 1 lb, for medium, use 1½ lb and approx 1 gallon of water as in method.

Chop or mince the sultanas and put them in fermenting vessel with half the sugar. Pour on 7 pints of boiling water and stir well to dissolve the sugar. Allow mixture to cool and then add the strained grapefruit juice. Mix well and add the tea, Pectozyme, yeast and nutrient. Cover as advised and leave to ferment for 8–9 days, stirring daily.

After this, strain and wring out tightly and return strained wine to cleaned fermenting vessel. Boil remaining sugar in 1 pint of water for 2 minutes and, when it has cooled, add it to the rest. Cover as before and leave for a further 3–4 days.

Then pour carefully into a gallon jar leaving as much deposit behind as you can. The next step is to fill up the jar with cooled boiled water to where the neck begins, fit a fermentation lock and leave until all fermentation has ceased.

Dried Currant Wine

Dried currants are another fruit best used for medium or
sweet wines. Something about their rather special flavour does
not go well in truly dry wines.
2½ lb currants, 3 oranges, 2 lemons, ¼ pint strong tea, ½ teaspoonful Pectozyme, sugar: for medium, use 1¾ lb, for sweet,
use 2¼ lb, yeast of your choice, nutrient and approx 1 gallon
of water as in method.
Chop or mince the currants and put them in fermenting
vessel with half the sugar and pour on 7 pints boiling water
stirring well to dissolve the sugar. Allow the mixture to cool
and grate the orange peel into the vessel. Then add the
strained juice of both oranges and lemons. Add the tea, yeast,
nutrient and Pectozyme. Then cover as advised and leave to
ferment for 10 days, stirring daily.

After this, strain and wring out tightly and return strained
wine to cleaned fermenting vessel. Boil remaining sugar in 1
pint of water for 2 minutes and, when it has cooled, mix it
into the rest. Cover as before and leave for a further 3–4 days.

Having done this, pour carefully into a gallon jar leaving
as much deposit behind as you can. Fill up the jar with cooled
boiled water to where the neck begins, fit a fermentation lock
and leave until all fermentation has ceased.

Dried Apricot Wine

Very good dry to medium wines are easily made with this
fruit but as sweet wines they seem to lack flavour. Using
more fruit to obtain more flavour is not the answer so we
must say that these are best used for dry to medium wines.
2 lb dried apricots, ½ lb sultanas, ¼ pint freshly made strong
tea, 1 lemon, ½ teaspoonful Pectozyme, yeast of your choice,
nutrient, sugar: for dry, use 2 lb, for medium, use 2¾ lb, and
water as in method.
Put the apricots in 7 pints of water and allow to soak overnight. Bring to boil and simmer gently with the lid on until
tender.

Put the chopped sultanas in fermenting vessel with half the sugar and pour on the simmering apricots. Stir well for several minutes and, when it has cooled, crush the apricots.

Add the tea, strained juice of the lemon and the grated rind of this and then add the Pectozyme, yeast and nutrient. Cover as advised and leave to ferment for 8 days, stirring daily.

After this, strain and wring out tightly and return strained wine to cleaned fermenting vessel. Boil remaining sugar in 1 pint of water for 2 minutes and, when it has cooled, add it to the rest. Cover as before and leave to ferment for a further 3–4 days.

After this, pour carefully into a gallon jar leaving as much deposit behind as you can. Then fill up the jar with cooled boiled water to where the neck begins, fit a fermentation lock and leave until all fermentation has ceased.

Dried Elderberry Wine

Dried elderberries are a boon to those not in easy reach of them and they make excellent wines. Dry, medium or sweet may be made with top-class results assured but do make sure before you begin that you will like this as a dry wine.

NOTE: Elderberries must be washed thoroughly under a running tap, so put them in a muslin cloth supported by a colander. They are very small and can be easily washed away. Thorough washing is essential otherwise the flavour of the wine will be marred.

For dry. ½ *lb dried elderberries,* ½ *lb sultanas,* 3 *lemons,* 2 *lb sugar,* ½ *teaspoonful Pectozyme, yeast of your choice, nutrient and approx* 1 *gallon of water as in method.*

For medium. ½ *lb dried elderberries,* 1 *lb sultanas,* 3 *lemons,* 2½ *lb sugar,* ½ *teaspoonful Pectozyme, yeast of your choice, nutrient and approx* 1 *gallon of water as in method.*

For sweet. ¾ *lb dried elderberries,* 1 *lb raisins,* 3 *lemons,* 3 *lb sugar,* ½ *teaspoonful Pectozyme, yeast of your choice, nutrient and approx* 1 *gallon of water as in method.*

Put the elderberries in fermenting vessel with the chopped dried fruits. Boil half the sugar in 7 pints of water for 2 minutes and while boiling pour over the fruits.

Allow to cool thoroughly. Then grate the lemon rind into the mixture and then add the strained juice. Having done this, add the yeast, nutrient and Pectozyme, cover as advised and leave to ferment for 7 days, stirring and crushing the pulp daily.

Then strain and wring out tightly and return strained wine to cleaned fermenting vessel. Boil remaining sugar in 1 pint of water (use ½ pint of water if sweet wine is being made) for 2 minutes and when cool add to the rest. Cover as before and leave for a further 6–7 days.

After this, pour carefully into a gallon jar leaving as much deposit behind as you can. Fill up the jar with cooled boiled water to where the neck begins, fit a fermentation lock and leave until all fermentation has ceased.

Dried Bilberry Wine

Three top-class types of wines may be made with dried bilberries. And as with dried elderberries, these must be washed very thoroughly before use.

For dry. An excellent claret. 1 *lb dried bilberries*, 1 *lb sultanas*, 3 *lemons*, 1½ *lb sugar*, ½ *teaspoonful Pectozyme, yeast of your choice, nutrient and approx* 1 *gallon of water as in method.*

For medium. 1¼ *lb bilberries*, 1 *lb raisins*, 3 *lemons*, 2½ *lb sugar*, ½ *teaspoonful Pectozyme, yeast of your choice and approx* 1 *gallon of water as in method.*

For sweet. 1½ *lb dried bilberries*, 1 *lb raisins*, 3 *lemons*, ½ *teaspoonful Pectozyme*, 3 *lb sugar, yeast of your choice, nutrient and approx* 1 *gallon of water as in method.*

Put the bilberries in fermenting vessel with the chopped dried fruit. Boil half the sugar in 7 pints of water for 2 minutes and while it is boiling pour it over the fruits. When it has cooled, grate the rind of the lemons over the mixture and add the strained juice. Then add the yeast, nutrient and Pectozyme. Cover as advised and leave to ferment for 10 days, stirring daily.

Having done this, strain and wring out tightly and return strained wine to cleaned fermenting vessel. Boil remaining sugar in 1 pint of water for 2 minutes (use ½ pint of water if making sweet wine), and when cool add to the rest. Cover again as before and leave for a further 3–4 days.

Then pour carefully into a gallon jar leaving as much deposit behind as you can. Fill up the jar with cooled boiled water to where the neck begins, fit a fermentation lock and leave until all fermentation has ceased.

The sweet will need keeping for a year or two to be at its best.

Chapter 13

MAKING WINES FROM TINNED FRUITS

I have known for a long time that tinned fruits sold in shops would eventually find themselves earmarked by enterprising housewives for winemaking purposes. I did a little experimenting with this type of winemaking a few years ago but other ingredients were so abundant that I really felt that it was hardly worth my while because I had plenty of other stuff for the asking.

But this is not the case with everybody. There are many people seeking means of making wines from ready at hand ingredients that resemble the wines they would make if they could grow the fruit for themselves. But this convenience in obtaining the ingredients does not seem to be the overriding factor. It seems to me that many people obtain such excellent results – and I know I have done so myself – with this type of ingredient that they would rather use them than use fresh fruit. I cannot see that these can make wines better than fresh garden fruits but I am able to agree that they would most likely make better wines than those made from fruit that has hung about in shops for perhaps a week or more.

The following recipes will be found useful by those who want to try their hand at what will doubtless be a new style of winemaking for them. Bear in mind that tinned fruits have been heated which means that active pectin will be present – thus we shall have to use a pectin-destroying enzyme as in many other cases. Remember too that most fruits today – except pineapple – are tinned in heavy syrup, so a little less sugar is needed.

This however has been taken care of in the recipes so it need not bother you.

The following method is suitable for all the recipes in this chapter. Follow this carefully and I am sure you will be just as pleased with the results as I have been myself.

As I have not carried out trials with pie fillings and various purées with which some people make wines, I cannot give recipes for these. In any case, I have the fancy that most of these are made mainly from the residue of the presses of fruit juice manufacturers, which means that most of the flavour and goodness have been taken out of them. I may be wrong.

So I give you recipes only for those I can be sure of.

NOTE: Additional acid is not normally required since I have found that the amounts of fruit used give enough into the wine. However, you can taste the must before you add the yeast and nutrient and judge for yourself whether there is enough for your liking or not. Alternatively, you can wait until the wine is nearly finished and then sample and add a small amount if you want to. Do not wait until the wine is completely finished before deciding about this.

It will be seen in the recipes that I recommend 15-oz tins. Some manufacturers vary their weight content slightly, so half or an ounce either way will not matter. Caterers suppliers make larger tins which would be far more economical in price.

Method. Put the fruit in the fermentation vessel and crush well by hand. Boil half the sugar in 6 pints of water and, when it has cooled somewhat but not necessarily completely, pour over the fruit.

The mixture should be cool enough to add the yeast right away but make sure of this. Then add yeast, nutrient, tea and Pectozyme.

Cover as advised and leave to ferment for 8 days, stirring daily. After this, strain and press out as dry as you can and return strained wine to cleaned fermenting vessel.

Boil remaining sugar in 1 pint of water for 2 minutes and when cooled add to the rest. Cover again as before and leave for a further 3–4 days. Then pour carefully into a gallon jar leaving as much deposit behind as you can. If the jar is not filled to where the neck begins, fill to this level with cooled boiled water. Then fit a fermentation lock and leave until all fermentation has ceased.

Tinned Plum Wine

Top-class dry, medium or sweet wines may be made with these.

For dry. Two 15-oz tins plums, 1¾ lb sugar, ¼ pint freshly made strong tea, ½ teaspoonful Pectozyme, yeast of your choice, nutrient and water as in method.

For medium. Two 15-oz tins plums, 2½ or 2¾ lb sugar depending on whether you want medium dry or medium sweet, ¼ pint freshly made strong tea, ½ teaspoonful Pectozyme, yeast of your choice, nutrient and water as in method.

For sweet. Three 15-oz tins plums, 3 lb sugar, ¼ pint freshly made strong tea, ½ teaspoonful Pectozyme, yeast of your choice, nutrient and water as in method.

Tinned Pear Wine

Best to make two sorts with these, dry to medium sweet.

For dry. Two 15-oz tins pears, 2 lb sugar, ¼ pint freshly made strong tea, ½ teaspoonful Pectozyme, yeast of your choice, nutrient and water as in method.

For medium. Two and a half 15-oz tins pears, ¼ pint freshly made strong tea, 2¼ lb sugar, ½ teaspoonful Pectozyme, yeast of your choice, nutrient and water as in method.

Tinned Apricot Wine

I recommend dry to medium dry, as I have found these to

be best, but include a recipe for those who must have them sweet.

For dry. One and a half 15-oz tins apricots, 2 lb sugar, ¼ pint freshly made strong tea, ½ teaspoonful Pectozyme, yeast of your choice, nutrient and water as in method.

For medium. Two 15-oz tins apricots, 2½ lb sugar, ¼ pint freshly made strong tea, ½ teaspoonful Pectozyme, yeast of your choice, nutrient and water as in method.

For sweet. Two and a half 15-oz tins apricots, 2¾ lb sugar, ¼ pint freshly made strong tea, ½ teaspoonful Pectozyme, yeast of your choice, nutrient and water as in method.

Tinned Peach Wine

In my view best made dry to medium, but may be made sweet if you insist. Follow exactly the recipes for apricot wines but use half a 15-oz tin more in each case. This is necessary because peaches are slightly less strongly flavoured than apricots.

Tinned Prune Wines

Dry, medium or sweet may be made with excellent results assured but acid is needed with this fruit.

For dry. Two 15-oz tins prunes, 1½ lb sugar, juice of 2 lemons, ¼ pint freshly made strong tea, ½ teaspoonful Pectozyme, yeast of your choice, nutrient and water as in method.

For medium. Two 15-oz tins prunes, 2¼ lb sugar, juice of 2 lemons, ¼ pint freshly made strong tea, ½ teaspoonful Pectozyme, yeast, nutrient and water as in method.

For sweet. Three 15-oz tins prunes, 2¾ lb sugar, juice of 3 *lemons, ¼ pint freshly made strong tea, ½ teaspoonful Pecto-zyme, yeast, nutrient and water as in method.*

NOTE: the measures given as half 15-oz tins. If you find it more convenient to use smaller tins rather than to split a large one, by all means do so. It may well be that tin sizes vary in different areas but all you would have to do if you come across this would be to obtain smaller or larger tins to give you the overall number of ounces required. If you happen to add an ounce too much fruit it will not matter. So do not painstakingly measure divided amounts to the last ounce.

The acid (as lemon juice) in the prune recipe should be strained (if necessary) and added before the yeast is put in.

Experimenting with tinned fruit

Now that these recipes have appeared, many of you will want to try out your own ideas and these will most likely take the form of adding dried fruits. If you do this, the method will have to be altered slightly. But all you would have to do would be to chop the dried fruit, raisins or sultanas, and to put these in the fermenting vessel. The boiling syrup (sugar water) would then be poured over while boiling and when the mixture had cooled the tinned fruit would be added. Thereafter the process would be the same as in the method.

Bear in mind that raisins and sultanas contain approximately 50 per cent sugar, so you would need half a pound less sugar for each one pound of dried fruit added. If you were to reduce the amount of tinned fruit when using these you would have to add some acid to counterbalance the reduction there would be if less fruit were used.

Chapter 14

MAKING WINES FROM FLOWERS

Because flowers for winemaking are less easy to come by these days and because so many other ingredients are available, there is a certain amount of loss of interest in this form of winemaking but only amongst those making wine in the larger towns. Those living in areas where the flowers are available in abundance and at one's elbow, as it were, are still ardent fans of flower wines.

As mentioned at the beginning of this book, the countless people who write to me are looking for good wines that cost as little as possible. They know that the ingredients used a century ago can make good wines but they also know that the methods of a century ago did not produce such good results as they might.

Flowers make wines the like of which you could not hope to buy anywhere at the price. Other ingredients make top-class wines that hold their own with commercial products but flowers make fragrantly flavoured wines the like of which commercial producers could not hope to imitate.

It is agreed that making wines with flowers means collecting them instead of buying ready packed or bottled stuff. Nevertheless, the wines are certainly worth the hour or so needed to collect enough flowers to make several gallons.

As with most other ingredients I have been carrying out trials with flowers using ordinary sugar, honey instead of sugar and now with what is known as synthetic must. This is a German invention with the trade name of *Dold Kunstmostansatz*. Designed as it is to make a very light dry wine in its own right without other ingredients added it is very easily adapted to other uses.

A bottle costing about 20p will make two gallons of light dry wine of some character. Because this stuff ferments readily and has little of the kind of flavour that would spoil other flavours, I decided to see what the result would be of using a small amount of this must as a basic fermentable medium while using flowers to give the necessary flavour and aroma.

The must itself is balanced to make two gallons but we shall be using only a quarter bottle in making a gallon of wine. Because we will be using only half the required amount, we must still add some acid and tannin to balance the deficiency. If we used this must at its full strength the flavour and aroma given into the wines by the flowers would be marred.

Although honey is used in certain recipes instead of sugar where flowers are being used, I have found that ordinary sugar is best where the must is also being employed. The part the must plays is that it gives a freshness into the wine that would otherwise be lacking.

When measuring the flowers according to the amount required in a recipe, use a pint or a quart jug, put in the flowers or petals and merely bump the jug on a suitable surface to settle them. On no account press them down by hand otherwise too many flowers will be used.

In old recipes – and indeed in many modern ones – more flowers are recommended than in these ones. However, I have found that the amounts in these recipes are sufficient, taking into account that we are using a basic ingredient as well.

Flowers growing on bushes or trees are merely pulled off into a suitable container such as a basket. Dandelions must be gathered on a sunny day (otherwise you will not find any), and the heads only, with not the tiniest part of the stem, should be taken. If stem is taken, the bitter 'milk' may contaminate the petals.

When gathered, dandelions close up. This means that when making the wine all you do is to hold the green part in one hand and pull out all the petals in one go with the other, only the petals being used.

Flowers do not make satisfactory sweet wine, so we must settle for dry or medium in all cases. The one method below is suitable for all the recipes in this chapter so there is no need to repeat it after each recipe. Merely decide which wine you want to make, select the appropriate recipe and work it as follows:

Method for all Flower Wines

Put the flowers in the fermenting vessel. Boil half the sugar in 6 pints of water for 2 minutes and while very hot pour over the flowers and cover immediately. When it has cooled, add the strained lemon juice, tea, nutrient, yeast and synthetic must. Cover as advised for all other wines and ferment for 8 days, stirring daily.

After 4 days, peel the bananas, discard the peel, pulp the bananas and boil them for 5 minutes in 1 pint of water. When this has cooled, add to the rest and add the Pectozyme. Cover again as before and after 8 days strain and wring out tightly and return strained wine to cleaned fermenting vessel.

Boil remaining sugar in ½ pint of water for two minutes and when it has cooled, add it to the rest. Leave covered as before for a further 3–4 days.

After this, pour carefully into a gallon jar leaving as much deposit behind as you can. Fill up the jar with cooled boiled water to where the neck begins, fit a fermentation lock and leave until all fermentation has ceased.

NOTE: In case you want to know what the Pectozyme is for, there is a risk that boiling the bananas – which is essential – might give rise to pectin cloud in the finished wine. So I recommend Pectozyme to avoid this possibility.

Dandelion Wine

Dry or medium. Aromatic wines of some character when kept a long time. The dry does not improve so much as the medium, so this may be used sooner.

2 *quarts petals*, ¼ *pint strong tea*, 2 *lemons*, ¼ *bottle synthetic must, sugar: for dry, use* 2 *lb, and for medium, use* 2¾ *lb*, 3 *fully ripe bananas*, ¼ *teaspoonful Pectozyme, yeast of your*

choice, nutrient and approx 1 gallon of water as in method.

Rose Petal Wine

Rose petals make delightfully aromatic wines of distinction. *4 pints rose petals, ¼ pint strong tea, ¼ bottle synthetic must, 2 lemons, sugar: for dry, use 2 lb, and for medium, use 2¾ lb, 3 fully ripe bananas, ¼ teaspoonful Pectozyme, yeast of your choice, nutrient and approx 1 gallon of water as in method.*

Gorse Wine

Exceptional wines may be made with gorse flowers. Pale golden and delightfully aromatic, these are wines you should be proud of when made well.
3 quarts gorse flowers, ¼ pint strong tea, ¼ bottle synthetic must, 2 lemons, sugar: for dry, use 2 lb, for medium, use 2¾ lb and for sweet, use 3 lb (and another quart of flowers), 3 fully ripe bananas, ¼ teaspoonful Pectozyme, yeast of your choice, nutrient and approx 1 gallon of water as in method.

Elderflower Wine

Fewer flowers are needed here owing to the pungency of the fragrance.
1–1½ pints elderflowers, ¼ pint strong tea, ¼ bottle synthetic must, 2 lemons, sugar: for dry, use 2 lb, and for medium, use 2¾ lb, 3 fully ripe bananas, ¼ teaspoonful Pectozyme, yeast of your choice, nutrient and approx 1 gallon of water as in method.

If fresh flowers are not available you may use a 2-oz packet of the dried sort from a dealer in home winemaking ingredients.

Hawthorn Flower Wine

(May blossom.) The hedgerows are usually white with these blossoms in May and even into June.

1–1½ *pints hawthorn blossom*, ¼ *pint strong tea*, ¼ *bottle synthetic must*, 2 *lemons, sugar: for dry, use 2 lb, and for medium, use* 2¾ *lb*, 3 *fully ripe bananas*, ¼ *teaspoonful Pectozyme, yeast of your choice, nutrient and approx 1 gallon of water as in method.*

Chapter 15

MAKING WINES FROM GRAPES

Outdoor grape growing is very much on the increase at the present time for it has at last been brought home to gardeners that vines are easy to grow in this country. They do well, either in the open garden, against walls or under cloches. Furthermore, they are not expensive to buy and need practically nothing by way of fertilizers.

At the time of writing, a worthwhile vine costs about £1.25 and in a couple of years will produce enough grapes for several gallons of wine. A few years later, it will produce many more. This is not the place for details about vines but just let me say that anybody with a small garden that gets plenty of sun can grow grapes as easily as any other fruit.

Making wines with grapes is probably the easiest of winemaking. This is because recipes are not needed. All one has to do is to crush the grapes and ferment them as one would any other wine.

You can take any variety of grape and rely on it making a top-class wine. But, and this is the most important part, you must choose the grape that will make the sort of wine you are likely to need. Those sold in shops, although somewhat expensive, will always make good wines to suit the average palate. Sweet or moderately sweet black grapes will make for dry to medium sweet wines but it is doubtful whether your home-grown grapes will turn out sweet wines. Some sugar will have to be added where these are required. Green, sweet grapes will also make dry to medium sweet wines but these, of course, will be white wines.

Those who wish to grow grapes should choose the vine that will produce the kind of wine required; if desired the characteristics of this wine can be changed by adding sugar or other fruits.

It is all a matter of common sense and experience. Experience will show you what can be done and your common sense will show you how to do it. Anybody with a little experience in making wines with garden and hedgerow fruits should become expert at handling their own grapes in a very short while.

As mentioned, most grapes grown outdoors in this country and those bought in shops with perhaps the exception of the very sweet sorts from the Cape and other parts will make dry to medium sweet wines. It is obvious that if you want sweet wines you will have to add sugar and because you will not know how much sugar your grapes contain, you will have to crush them first and use the hydrometer to find how much sugar the juice contains.

On the whole, you should obtain a reading of about 1·070 from most grapes. And from some you might obtain a reading of as much as 1·090. Either way, this is not enough for sweet wines but it is enough for very dry wines of a reasonable alcohol content for this type. As mentioned earlier, dry wines are always better for being lower in alcohol.

Obviously, whichever type of wine you want to make, it would be wise to use the hydrometer to ascertain the sugar content so that you may adjust this if you want to. The hydrometer table on page 57 shows how much alcohol you will make with the various hydrometer readings. Details of using the hydrometer are included in the appropriate chapter.

From the hydrometer table you will decide on how much alcohol you want to make and add sugar accordingly. If for example you obtain a juice which gives you a reading of 1·080, and you want to make more alcohol than this reading will give you, you will have to add sugar, bearing in mind that $2\frac{1}{4}$ oz will raise the gravity by 5° on the hydrometer.

If you want a sweet wine, you will have to increase the gravity to something like 1·120 or even a bit more according to how sweet you like your wines.

However, as we have seen in the Hydrometer chapter, starting with a gravity higher than 1·110 is not a good practice. Therefore, if you are making sweet wines it is best to take the reading when detailed in the method which follows and then bring the reading up to 1·110 by adding sugar. You can rely on this amount of sugar being fermented out to give you the amount of alcohol you want for a sweet wine. Then, later, when the reading has dropped to about 1·060, add the sugar required to sweeten the wine. The amount to add must relate to personal tastes – it may be two ounces or it could be as much as ten. On the whole, I would advise you not to add more than four to six oz during the process of fermentation and then, when the wine is finished, sweeten a little more if necessary.

This applies mainly, of course, to your first attempt, for it is from this that you will learn just how much sugar is needed to make the wine sweet enough for your particular palate. So remember, when making dry wines, do not add sugar unless you must for bone-dry wines are better for being low in alcohol.

How many grapes make for a gallon of wine is a frequent question to which I always have to reply that it depends on the juice content.

Generally, anything between fifteen and twenty pounds are needed, so it is wise to begin with at least twenty pounds.

Method

Do not strip from the stalks, but put the whole bunches into the fermenting vessel and crush well by hand: add Campden solution (see p 60) and leave covered for an hour.

Take a sample of the must into a jug and strain it free of pips and skins and nearly fill the hydrometer flask with this. Slide the hydrometer into the sample and stand the flask on a level surface. Take the reading and calculate whether sugar is needed or not and then work out how much is needed if required.

Dissolve this in as little hot water as possible and then stir into the bulk. Give the mixture a thorough stirring and add the yeast of your choice.

Cover as advised on page 60 and leave to ferment for 10 days, stirring daily.

The next step is to wring out the pulp as dry as possible and to put the strained wine into cleaned fermenting vessel.

Pressing out the juice is a man's job with grapes and if you are likely to be making two or three gallon batches or more it would be wise to invest in a small press which will last a lifetime.

If any sweetening sugar is to be added it is best to add it now, or at least a proportion of it as already discussed.

Cover again as before and leave for a further 3–4 days. Then transfer to a jar leaving as much deposit behind as you can. *Do not* add water to fill the jar. If you have a little more than a gallon, set this aside in a separate container just large enough to hold it and plug the neck with cotton wool. As the level in the jar falls, top up with this.

Having filled the jar, fit a fermentation lock and leave until all fermentation ceases but top up with surplus if you have it. If not, leave the wine as it is.

The process thereafter is the same as for any other wine.

Chapter 16

MAKING WINES FROM
CONCENTRATED GRAPE JUICES

Using concentrated grape juices has become very popular in recent years and I imagine that their popularity will continue to grow unless they become too expensive. The wide popularity they enjoy today is because they are relatively inexpensive, easy to handle, ready to use and give top-class results.

A quart of concentrate costs about 63p if you shop for it yourself, otherwise postage must be added to the cost. Either way, one usually turns out a top-class wine at about 75p a gallon or perhaps just a bit more. Those without gardens and not within easy reach of wild fruits find concentrated grape juices an absolute boon: coming as they do from many parts of the continent and North Africa as well as Cyprus, there is a wide enough range to choose from and it is the matter of choosing the concentrate that will give the results most likely to meet your needs which is important.

I have used most of those available including the most recent addition to one firm's range designed to make an excellent hock. This is achieved by the firm blending the grape juice and I have been absolutely delighted with the results. And not only with the results of this particular concentrate but with all of them.

My advice to anybody deciding to use these is to obtain two or three varieties in quarts or half-gallons and to use them all at once or as near after each other as you can. In this way you will be able to have on hand several different types and to be able to choose which you prefer. The chances are that you will have great difficulty in deciding which you like best for the very simple reason that they will all be first-class wines of their kind.

It is just as easy to make these dry or sweet as it is with any other wine. And while, strictly speaking, there is no need to use the hydrometer when using grape concentrates for dry wines, it is often advisable to use it whether you are making dry or sweet wines.

The reason for this is that the concentrate is advertised as having a certain specific gravity – usually around 1·380 or 1·400, or somewhere between the two. It is important to find out for sure whether this is in fact true. It will not be far off but far enough to throw out of balance a particular wine where a certain degree of dryness or sweetness is required.

Now let us look at those figures 1·380 and 1·400. As I have explained in the hydrometer chapter, only the figure above the one thousand (1·) need concern us as this represents the sugar content. So whatever the specific gravity of the grape juice you buy, you must concern yourself only with the figure above. I repeat this because the concentrate you get hold of may be claimed to have a different specific gravity to the two figures quoted.

One quart of concentrate makes one gallon of wine while one gallon makes four gallons of wine. So all one has to do is to make one quart into one gallon by adding water. It will be seen that we increase the volume to four times what it was. However, we must be accurate here, so go carefully. If, as we have seen, we increase the volume by four times, we automatically reduce the specific gravity to a fourth of what it was. Therefore, the figure above the one thousand is divided by four and you know from this what the specific gravity of your diluted juice, ready for fermenting, will be.

In the case of the specific gravity 1·380, the reading when reduced to a quarter would be 1·095 and, for the reading of 1·400, the diluted reading would be 1·100.

If you take a look at the hydrometer table you will at once see how much alcohol these amounts of sugar (specific gravities) will make and it is for you to decide whether you want to make more alcohol or not. Just let me say that if you are making dry wine the amount of alcohol that will be made with these amounts of sugar is plenty.

However, as I have mentioned, the figures quoted by the supplier are not always correct and for this reason it is as well to use the hydrometer.

But first, make a quart of concentrate into exactly one gallon or half a gallon into two gallons or a gallon into four gallons and then take the reading using a hydrometer reading from 1·000 to 1·100. When you have found the true specific gravity of the diluted juice you may add more sugar if you want to. Mix the concentrate thoroughly with the water otherwise you will not get an accurate reading. Bear in mind that two and a quarter ounces of sugar will raise the reading 5° on the hydrometer. Therefore, if you are making medium sweet or sweet wines and want to raise the reading say 15°, you will have to add three times two and a quarter ounces.

The best plan when making wines with concentrated grape juices is to boil the required water beforehand and to let it cool before mixing the concentrate with it. The concentrate is usually sterile, product free of any of the causes of spoilage that we have already discussed. This is not necessarily the case with our water supply which often contains wild yeast.

Alternatively, you may treat the three quarts of water for mixing with the concentrate with one Campden tablet as already described in the chapter on making wines by the Campden method.

If sugar has to be added, it will do no harm to put this in a saucepan with a very small amount of water and dissolve it by slowly bringing to the boil. When cool it may be added and mixed well with the prepared mixture. Yeast is then added together with nutrient and the whole fermented and treated as in any other wine. There will not be any need to strain these wines as there will not be any solids.

After ten or twelve days or when fermentation is seen to have slowed down, the wine is poured into a gallon jar and a fermentation lock fitted in the usual way. When using concentrates I think it by far the best plan to make two-gallon lots. This allows for a gallon jar to be filled as well as a half-gallon jar and the remainder allowed to ferment in a smaller container, all of which must, of course, be fitted with fermentation locks.

Then, as the level in the larger containers falls owing to the sugar being used up, a little may be added to the larger vessels to keep them filled. If this is done often you will find that you obtain one and a half gallons (nine bottles at bottling time).

These two may be used as required or added to another batch as topping up material.

Whichever way you work, and you will develop your own style or method, you will have some really first-class wines.

When you have made your first couple of batches using concentrated grape juices and have got the hang of using the hydrometer, you will find it all so easy that you will wonder why I had to explain it all in the first place.

Chapter 17

MAKING MEAD

This is one of the oldest known alcoholic drinks and certainly one of the finest. Made almost entirely of honey and water it is one of the easiest wines to make. Sweet dry or medium honey always makes wines of distinction and character which may be of the palest gold to an almost copper-bronze.

This is so popular today that commercial producers make and retail it in off-licences at about ten times the price you can make it yourself.

Even the continent imports British-made mead – the Germans in particular have a special regard for it.

There is no doubt that the very finest meads are made from pure English honey direct from the comb. But this is hard to come by these days unless you happen to know an apiarist. Pure English honeys are sometimes available in small jars in local shops in country areas, but the price asked puts making mead from it out of reach of most people. And because more and more bee-keepers are selling their honey to firms who blend it with other honeys in order to market a uniform product, pure English honeys as we used to know them will be a thing of the past quite soon.

There is no doubt that each individual honey makes its own special type of mead, but as we are not now likely to obtain one type of honey – but a blend of several – we should choose the blend as carefully as possible, even though the only clue that may be given is that the blend produces a mild flavoured or strong flavoured honey.

Strongly flavoured honey often produces a slightly harsh underlying flavour best avoided but a mildly flavoured honey will produce a mildly flavoured mead of good quality: the best way to buy is in bulk of at least 7 lb. This will produce up to 3 gallons of mead according to the type – dry or sweet – that you propose making.

As with all our ingredients, honey contains wild yeasts and bacteria and the wines made must be protected as for all other wines.

Sugar is never used when making mead. The honey itself consists mainly of approximately 75 per cent sugar. Therefore, all that is needed is to dilute the honey until the dilute mixture contains sufficient sugar for the type of wine required – sweet, dry, etc.

Generally speaking, 4 lb of honey will make for a sweet wine while 3 lb will make for a bone dry. Some acid and tannin will be needed in order to produce a reasonably well balanced must but all this is taken care of in the recipes.

Users of the hydrometer will be able to dilute their honey according to their requirements, but those not using this may follow the recipes with confidence.

Sweet Mead

4 lb honey, $\frac{1}{4}$ pint freshly made strong tea, $\frac{1}{4}$ oz citric acid (or $\frac{1}{8}$ oz each of citric and malic acid), 1 gallon of water, wine yeast of your choice or special mead yeast, and a good nutrient.

Dry Mead

Exactly as above using only 3 lb of honey.

Method

Put the measured honey in fermenting vessel and pour on all the water, mixing well in. Treat with $1\frac{1}{2}$ Campden tablets as directed for wine ($1\frac{1}{2}$ tablets are needed owing to starting with more than a gallon overall).

Leave well covered for an hour, then give a thorough stirring. Add the acid dissolved in a very small amount of warm water and add the tea; give a further stirring and then add the yeast.

Cover as advised for wines and leave to ferment for ten days or so. Then pour into a gallon jar and fit a fermentation lock.

The little that will not go into the jar may be put in a smaller container such as a wine bottle and kept plugged with cotton wool until the level in the jar falls, so that this extra may be added.

The wine is thereafter treated as all other wines. It may be that a heavy deposit will build up. If this happens, transfer to another jar leaving as much of this behind as you can and fill the new jar with the excess held over for the purpose; on no account add further water to top up the jar.

Chapter 18

MAKING WINES FROM UNCLASSIFIED INGREDIENTS

In other chapters the recipes are for wines made from a group of fruits or other ingredients. The recipes here cannot be put into these groups, so they must have a chapter to themselves.

The wines made by these recipes and ingredients are excellent wines but success here, as with others, is deciding for yourself in advance whether you are likely to like the wine made with any particular recipe and ingredient.

If you are doubtful and the ingredients are not expensive, it is always worthwhile making an experimental half-gallon batch to see if you like the result or not. But do bear in mind that a half-gallon batch will not make quite such good wines as will a gallon batch. This is because it very often happens that the bigger the batch the better the wine – up to a point. This is not to say that a fifty-gallon lot would be fifty times better than a one-gallon lot. It merely means that a three- or four-gallon lot will be better than a one-gallon lot. If this is so, you may well ask why all my recipes are for one gallon. The simple truth is that one-gallon lots are perfectly satisfactory and it is with this amount that most people like to get the feel of things. Once you have done this, you can adapt the recipe to make any amount you like merely by multiplying the amounts of all ingredients by the number of gallons you wish to make. To start off by making a five- or ten-gallon lot of a wine you are doubtful about and then find you do not like it would not be very sensible.

Pineapple Wine

Pineapple makes two excellent wines, medium sweet and dry. They are fresh, fruity and refreshing. I use two fifteen-oz tins, but you can use the equivalent in fresh pineapple if you want to though you may find it more expensive.

Two 15-oz tins pineapple, ½ lb sultanas, ¼ pint freshly made strong tea, sugar: for dry, use 2 lb, for medium, use 2¾ lb, yeast of your choice, nutrient and approx 1 gallon of water as in method.

Chop the sultanas and put them in fermenting vessel. Boil half the sugar in 6 pints of water for 2 minutes and while hot pour over the sultanas.

Allow mixture to cool and then add the pineapple, tea, yeast and nutrient. Cover as advised and leave to ferment for 10 days, stirring and pressing or crushing the pineapple chunks or slices as they become softened.

After 10 days, strain and wring out to ensure obtaining maximum juice and return strained wine to cleaned fermenting vessel. Boil remaining sugar in 1 pint water for 2 minutes and, when it has cooled, add it to the rest. Leave covered as before for a further 3–4 days.

Then pour carefully into a gallon jar leaving as much deposit behind as you can. Having done this, fill up the jar with cooled boiled water to where the neck begins, then fit a fermentation lock and leave until all fermentation has ceased.

Raisin and Tangerine Wine

Three very good wines of quite unique flavour may be made from this combination. Whether dry, medium or sweet, they arouse interest wherever they are sampled.

10–12 tangerines, 1½ lb raisins, ¼ pint freshly made strong tea, sugar: for dry, use 1¼ lb, for medium, use 2 lb, for sweet, use 2¼ lb, yeast, nutrient and approx 1 gallon of water as in method.

NOTE: For the dry, use 10 tangerines.

Chop the raisins and put them in fermenting vessel. Boil half the sugar in 6 pints of water for 2 minutes and while hot pour over the raisins.

Peel tangerines, discard the peel and crush the fruit. Add fruit to the raisins when the mixture is cool and then add the yeast, nutrient and tea. Cover as advised and leave to ferment for 8 days, stirring and crushing by hand daily.

Then strain and wring out tightly and return strained wine to cleaned fermenting vessel. Boil remaining sugar in 1 pint of water for 2 minutes and, when it has cooled, add it to the rest. Cover again as before and leave for a further 3–4 days.

Having done this, pour carefully into a gallon jar leaving as much deposit behind as you can. Then fill up the jar with cooled boiled water to where the neck begins, fit a fermentation lock and leave until all fermentation has ceased.

Rose-hip and Fig Wine

This one is best made as a dry wine and provided you like them dry you will be pleasantly surprised with the results.
6 oz dried rose-hip shells, 6 oz figs, 2 lb sugar, 2 lemons, ¼ pint freshly made strong tea, yeast of your choice, nutrient and approx 1 gallon of water as in method.

Wash the rose-hip shells thoroughly, chop or cut the figs up small and put them both in fermenting vessel.

Boil all the sugar in 7 pints of water for 2 minutes and while hot pour over the ingredients in the vessel. Allow mixture to cool, grate the lemon rind into the mixture and then add the strained lemon juice. Add the tea, yeast and nutrient. Cover as advised and leave to ferment for 10 days, stirring daily.

After this, strain and wring out dry and return strained wine to cleaned fermenting vessel. Cover again as before and leave for a further 3–4 days.

Then pour carefully into a gallon jar leaving as much deposit behind as you can. Fill up the jar with cooled boiled water to where the neck begins, then fit a fermentation lock and leave until all fermentation has ceased.

Raisin and Grapefruit Wine

This combination makes two excellent wines of the dry to medium sorts. It does not make a good sweet wine owing to the slight acidity that one must have in a wine made with grapefruit. These wines are excellent appetizers, though they may be used at other times.

6 *grapefruits, 2 lb raisins, ¼ pint strong tea, sugar: for dry, use 1 lb, for medium, use 2 lb, yeast of your choice, nutrient and approx 1 gallon of water as in method.*

NOTE: Pectozyme is not required.

Chop or mince the raisins and put them in fermenting vessel. Boil half the sugar in 6 pints of water for 2 minutes and while still boiling pour over the raisins. When mixture has cooled, add the tea and the strained grapefruit juice. Remove pips from the grapefruit pulp and then add the pulp to the mixture. Add pips and skins. Add yeast and nutrient. Cover as advised and leave to ferment for 10 days, stirring daily and pushing the cake of pips and skins under the surface.

After 10 days, strain and wring out tightly and return strained wine to cleaned fermenting vessel. Boil remaining sugar in 1 pint of water for 2 minutes and, when it has cooled, add it to the rest. Cover as before and leave to ferment for a further 3–4 days.

Then pour carefully into a gallon jar leaving as much deposit behind as you can. Having done this, fill up the jar with cooled boiled water to where the neck begins, fit a fermentation lock and leave until all fermentation has ceased.

Rose-hip and Grape Wine

Made as medium dry to dry, two good wines are to be had. Grape concentrate is used because it is easier to handle with this particular recipe.

6 *oz dried rose-hips, 1 pint white concentrated grape juice, 3 lemons, ¼ pint strong tea, sugar: for dry, use 1¼ lb, for*

medium, use 2¼ lb, yeast of your choice, nutrient and approx 1 gallon of water as in method.

NOTE: Very little sugar is required owing to the amount contained in the grape concentrate.

Thoroughly wash the rose-hips and put them with all the sugar in the fermenting vessel. Boil 7 pints of water and while boiling pour over the ingredients. Stir until sugar is dissolved and allow mixture to cool. Add concentrated grape juice and mix in. Then add the tea, strained juice of lemons, yeast and nutrient. Cover as advised and leave to ferment for 8 days, stirring daily.

After this, strain and wring out tightly and return strained wine to cleaned fermenting vessel. Cover again as before and leave for a further 3–4 days.

Then pour carefully into gallon jar leaving as much deposit behind as you can. Fill jar to where the neck begins with cooled boiled water, then fit a fermentation lock and leave until all fermentation has ceased.

A Final Word about Recipes

It is true to say that there are far too many recipes in circulation. It does not matter when a reader uses one book or several books by the same writer on the subject for, generally, the particular author has evolved the method that goes with the recipe and therefore all is well. But many people buy books by different writers on winemaking, then they find similar recipes with conflicting methods and it is here that they find that there are far too many recipes and perhaps methods as well. If he cares to analyse these, he will find that, basically, they are very similar, though the results vary quite a lot.

I could have doubled or trebled the number of recipes in this book merely by taking a couple of oranges away here or adding a couple of lemons there or, for example, where I recommend 2 pounds of one particular ingredient with 1 pound of another, by merely reversing this, the wines would have been different to those made with the recipes as they stand – not a great deal perhaps, but different all the same.

But what is the point of all this: with a confusion of similar yet slightly different recipes, the poor beginner has difficulty in knowing where to begin. Give him clear-cut recipes for dry, medium and sweet from each type of ingredient and he will know where he is.

One can very easily understand how this multitude of recipes has come about. One might even say 'thirty thousand ways with elderberries'. This would be a bit of an exaggeration but if we are not careful it will become true.

Obviously, what happens is that someone makes wine with a recipe and then decides that a little more of this would have made it even better; so next time he makes what alteration he wants and passes it on. The next chap does the same only in a different direction and he passes it on. The next bloke . . . And so it goes on, so that where there was one recipe there are now perhaps a dozen and even more being evolved from the original.

There are enough reliable recipes and methods in this book to last anybody a lifetime. You will not try them all because you will do the sensible thing. You will go for those recipes that will make the wine you think you will like most and then narrow your choice of preferences over the years to perhaps a dozen different types which you will make regularly and thus produce quality wines consistently.

Do bear in mind that when someone says 'Oh, you simply haven't lived until you've tried such and such a wine', if you make this yourself, it may be the worst wine you have ever tasted. Tastes vary so widely that you meet up with this sort of thing every day. It is the same with commercial products: while some people shudder at certain wines, others swear there is nothing to compare with them. So it's all a matter of making the wine you like. Among the recipes here there are a good many that will make the very sort of wines you have been looking for, so make a variety to start with and gradually – as you go along – decide which are really your types and which are not. Then start to build up a cellar of your favourites.

Chapter 19

BEWARE OF POISON PLANTS

At least one letter a week reaches me asking for a recipe for making wines from various plants and flowers. It is wise that people ask before embarking on their own because quite often they are thinking of making wines with plants that contain poisons.

This is not to say that the wine would necessarily contain sufficient poisons as to prove fatal or that enough would be present to cause serious stomach disorders. It could well be that the process of fermentation or the presence of sugar and alcohol would minimize their effects but we do not know for sure either way. It could be that the presence of certain substances produced during fermentation might well make them even more dangerous.

There appears to be a need for detailed research into this aspect, as it is obviously of great importance. It is well known for example that the leaves and stems of tomatoes and potatoes as well as the leaves of rhubarb are quite dangerous.

Certain animals can eat certain plants and berries while others will be killed by them. Rabbits, for example, eat and enjoy a certain type of fungus, yet the amount he can eat in one go would kill a family of five humans. A large number of examples could be given but these would not be altogether relevant.

I can say that even certain roots and fruits and the kernels of fruits are, at some time during their development stage, dangerous. However, by the time we eat them they are harmless or, if mild poisons still remain, other foods eaten at the same time or our own digestive systems render them harmless.

But this is not the case with all plants, berries, roots, and seeds. So these few notes are necessary. This is not the type of book for detailed analysis of plants, or how and why they are dangerous. Therefore I can give only a list of plants to avoid. I have it on authority besides my own personal experience that you should *not* make wines with the following materials:

Foxgloves,
Lily of the valley,
Yew berries,
Horse-chestnut (conkers),
Poppies,
Common privet,
Cyclamen,
Bryony,
Potatoes allowed to become green through exposure to air and light,
Buttercups,
Bluebells,
Lilac,
The nightshades,
Marsh marigold,
Honeysuckle,
Narcissus family (including daffodils),
Hyacinth,
Common broom,
Monkshood,
Wood anemone (as children we used to call these 'wooden enemies'),
Sweet pea,
Laburnum,
Rhododendrons,
Delphinium,
Clematis,
Verbena,
Thorn apple.

Those listed (or at least, most of them) are those that readers of my other books and magazine articles most often ask about.

If you want a good maxim, whenever you are thinking of making wines with ingredients you are doubtful about, just repeat to yourself: if a recipe for these can't be found, don't use them. In other words, if a recipe is not readily available, there is good reason for it.

Whenever you are gathering fruits from the hedgerows and fields and find others you are not sure of, leave them alone. Elderberries, blackberries, sloes, bilberries and other materials we gather from the wilds are so well known that there can be no mistaking them. But others are there and often strikingly attractive, and their attractiveness should be a warning in itself. So there it is: DO NOT MAKE WINES WITH ANY INGREDIENT YOU CANNOT FIND A RECIPE FOR. Heaven knows, there is surely a wide enough variety of ingredients available readily and cheaply, and very often conveniently and free into the bargain, without having to search round for something that might make the last bottle of wine you may ever drink.

Chapter 20

NEW WAYS WITH T'NOIROT EXTRACTS

Readers of my numerous other books will know that I am always looking for new and better ways of using all sorts of ingredients, and because I have known all along that T'noirot extracts offer something quite out of the ordinary, I have devoted more time to these than I have, perhaps, to any other sort of ingredient. This is not to say that I have neglected others for I have not, as readers of my other books will also know. I have evolved hundreds of new recipes and a new method or two for many of the more usual ingredients, not to mention carrying out trials with yeasts, certain sugars, nutrients, temperatures and many other aspects of wine-making.

I have written elsewhere a good deal about these extracts and have given many recipes for their use. But the recipes here are completely new and are the results of experiments that I have been carrying out over the past two years.

On the whole, these extracts are expensive compared with wild and garden fruit but very cheap when compared with certain dried fruits and concentrated grape juice. Unfortunately, while they *will* make wines when used with water, sugar and yeast only, they are very slow in doing so. It takes many many months to get fermentation to completion owing to lack of suitable organic matter.

But when used with comparatively inexpensive basic ingredients that put into the must the elements necessary for a full and complete fermentation, it is a very different story. Indeed, the recipes here, used with a good yeast and nutrient, should ferment as well as any well-balanced mixture prepared mainly from fresh fruit pulps.

With these, we must use a little acid and tannin, and also some Pectozyme in order to be doubly sure of not having a clearing problem.

T'noirot extracts are not concentrated flavourings in the strict meaning of the word. They are extracts of fruits and herbs blended to give the true flavours of the various liqueurs the names of which they carry. Amongst these are:

Red Curaçao,
White Curaçao,
Green Convent,
Yellow Convent,
Danzig,
Kummel,
Mirabelle,
Prunelle,
Cherry Brandy,
Sloe Gin,
Cream of Apricot,
Cream of Peach,
Vermouth – French or Italian.

A more detailed list may be had from the suppliers listed at the end of this book.

When carrying out my recent experiments with these extracts it was essential to produce a basic must that would ferment well and to completion whether the extract was to be added or not. This was because strictly speaking the extracts are not good fermentable medi alone.

It was also essential to produce a must with very little flavour of its own so that it could not alter in any way the flavour of the extract. From this it will be noted that these recipes would not make good wines without the extracts – so do not be tempted to try this. You would get wine of the usual alcohol content but of precious little flavour.

I have mentioned that these extracts are relatively expensive. But when one considers the type of wine that may be made they are, in effect, rather inexpensive. Vermouth, for example, would cost about 75p a gallon, which is a good deal less than the cost of a bottle. It is not difficult to obtain the effect – that is to say the correct desired colour for the product – with these because in most cases the extract will do this adequately.

Unfortunately, I cannot cover these extracts in such detail as I have elsewhere but I am able to give enough recipes for anyone to be able to use the extract of their choice.

In this respect I have evolved recipes that will not spoil the colour given into the wine by the extract.

For the paler coloured extracts the following recipe is recommended. These will produce pale coloured wines flavoured of whichever liqueur you use. Bear in mind that although you are producing liqueur-flavoured wine, they are still wines of the usual alcohol content.

Recipe for the paler coloured extracts

1 lb bananas, 1 lb sultanas, 2½ lb sugar, ¼ oz citric acid, ¼ oz tartaric acid, ¼ pint freshly made strong tea (or equivalent in grape tannin), ½ teaspoonful Pectozyme, 1 bottle extract of your choice, yeast of your choice, nutrient and water as in method.
NOTE: When ordering the extract, ask for the bottle size for one gallon of must.

Recipe for the darker coloured extracts

1 lb bananas, 1 lb raisins, 2½ lb sugar, ¼ oz citric acid, ¼ oz tartaric acid, ¼ pint freshly made strong tea (equivalent in grape tannin not needed as tea will add to the darker colour), ½ teaspoonful Pectozyme, 1 bottle extract of your choice, nutrient, yeast of your choice and water as in method.
NOTE: When ordering the extract, order the bottle size suitable for one gallon of must.

Darker and lighter coloured extract. To avoid having to give a list of extracts and their various colours, you may decide which recipe to use merely by holding the bottle of extract to light and then decide for yourself whether it is pale or dark. The only real difference is that one recipe makes for a lighter coloured wine which will suit the colour of the extract and the other a darker wine for the darker coloured extract.

Vermouth

This expensive commercial product is very easy to imitate with excellent results. The main difference between Italian and French being that Italian is sweeter than the French. For this wine, use the second recipe – that is the one containing raisins, but use half a pound less sugar for dry vermouth.

The method given below is suitable for both the recipes given and for whichever extract you wish to use.

Chop or mince the dried fruits and put them in fermenting vessel. Boil half the sugar in 5 pints of water for 2 minutes and while boiling pour over the fruit, mixing well together.

Allow mixture to cool a little and then add the acids and tea, stirring well in. When mixture is cooled well, add the extract of your choice, yeast, nutrient and Pectozyme.

Cover as advised and leave to ferment for 10 days, stirring daily. After 5 days, peel and pulp the bananas. Boil them for 10 minutes in 2 pints of water and when cooled add to the rest.

Cover as before and leave to ferment for the remainder of the 10 days.

Having done this, strain and wring out tightly and return strained wine to cleaned fermenting vessel. Boil remaining sugar in 1 pint of water for 2 minutes and when cooled add to the rest. Cover as before and leave for a further 3–4 days.

Transfer carefully to a gallon jar leaving as much deposit behind as you can. If the jar is not filled to where the neck begins, fill to this level with cooled boiled water, then fit a fermentation lock and leave until all fermentation has ceased. Thereafter the procedure is the same as for any other wine.

Do not taste wines made from these extracts while in the process of manufacture or, at least, not until fermentation has been going on for some time. This is because the extract is not diluted in the early stages as much as it will be when the jar is filled. For this reason, the flavour might, at the time of tasting, appear rather too strong. Experienced winemakers will not need this warning but the inexperienced never can resist popping in a finger and licking it just to see how things are coming along.

T'noirot extracts to the rescue. I think it perfectly safe to say that no one will be disappointed with any of the wine they will make from recipes in this book but it may well be that you already have a few bottles of earlier makes that are not up to expectations.

Provided these have sufficient acid and are brilliantly clear and that it is merely lack of flavour that is the fault, then T'noirot extracts will improve them. On no account try to alter the flavour of a fully flavoured wine with these otherwise you will waste the extract and ruin the wine. This is because so much extract would have to be used to obliterate the flavour of the wine that the overall effect would be quite awful.

But it is very easy to give almost any flavour you wish to any wine lacking flavour by using T'noirot extracts. Small bottles are obtainable especially for the purpose. These, like the larger bottle designed for making wines, cover the whole range of T'noirot flavours and it is for you to decide which you want to use.

When doing this, add a few drops of your chosen extract to your disappointing wine, mix well by shaking, sample just a tiny amount and add a drop or two more if necessary. Do this carefully because it is quite easy to overdo it.

Our grandparents were wizards at this sort of thing. They used to dose their disappointing wines with cloves, ginger and even allspice and because these all gave the impression to the palate that the wines were high in alcohol, most people used to imagine that they were a bit tipsy long before they actually were. But do not, I implore you, use cloves, ginger or other similar types of flavourings or spices as most of these ruin good wines.

However, if you would like to experiment with T'noirot extracts, I am sure you will enjoy the results. I say this because the recent additional extracts which have been added to the very wide range include rye whisky, dry gin, and Scotch whisky. These would make wonderful novelty wines for those who are interested in this sort of thing.

Do be careful, though, not to add these flavourings to wines they are not suitable for, for example red fruit wines or flower wines.

The gin and whisky flavourings would go very well with root wines whether they have a good flavour or not. Novelties of this sort are bound to stimulate interest and curiosity at parties and at Christmas time. Making up new sorts of wines should be easy enough after a little trial and error.

Chapter 21

WAYS OF SERVING WINE

You would think that having made decent wines it would come naturally how to serve and take them. 'Taking wines' is the sophisticated way of saying 'drinking wines' except that wines are never drunk – only taken.

Be that as it may, whether I am taking wines or drinking them seems not to matter, I enjoy them a great deal and would not be without them. As I have mentioned earlier, there is no place for snobbery in this hobby and I am not trying to instil snobbish ideas on how to serve or drink (sorry, take) your wines.

It is simply that wines served in certain types of glasses are better for being served in these glasses in the same way as various wines are more suitable for certain purposes.

The best glass to use for almost all wine types is undoubtedly the Parish Goblet, the five- or six-ounce size being ideal.

The thin glass of these allows you to warm the wine by cupping the bowl in the palms of the hands if you want the chill off. If you want it to remain cold you hold the glass by the stem. Thin clear glass also allows you to hold the wine to light to admire the many colours that are intermingled and which would not be noticeable in a thick glass or one that is coloured. The bowl shape allows the bouquet to collect itself for your enjoyment. The thin lips are a pleasure to your own lips. Filling the glass to a suitable level is far more important than most people imagine. It is common to see glasses filled to the very brim when in fact a glass three parts full is usually full enough.

How do you drink your wines and what you drink them with is a very personal matter and it is not for me to tell you that a certain wine must be taken with the fish and another taken with the pheasant, and so on. If you want to do the opposite to what was once considered 'the thing' then you are free to do so.

Many people drink their wines without ever thinking of taking a bit of bread and cheese with them but you would be surprised how good this combination is. I like to take a dry biscuit to nibble with a sweet red wine – try it, I am sure you will be delighted.

There are many ways of discovering how to get the best from your wines – the dry unsweetened biscuit with a sweet wine is only one of them. A cream cracker taken together with a dry wine is absolutely delightful. I mention only two examples so that you can try out your own ideas and whims. You will be astonished how many ideas spring to mind when you begin doing this sort of thing.

After all, we are not all of the 'knock 'em back and 'urry up with the next one' brigade. Most of us know that there is beauty in wine and that, like beauty in other things, it must be brought out to be enjoyed to the full.

So do try other means, apart from just drinking your wines, of finding the best way to get the very best out of them. I am sure you will be happy and delighted that you did.

Chapter 22

YOUR QUESTIONS ANSWERED

Despite the wide coverage in all my books, there are readers who have problems peculiar to themselves and which cannot be answered by dissecting the text. For this reason I include a cross-section of the many queries I receive from readers of my other books and monthly articles which appear in several magazines.

Q. I have been making wines for a number of years and have several glass jars which are badly stained a deep reddish-brown colour. The only wines put into these has been elderberry. Can you tell me how to get rid of this stain?

A. Elderberry wines will stain jars in this fashion. Put about a half-pint of unscented, soapless detergent into them – bleach such as Brobat is ideal – and then fill to the brim with water. The stain should soak off in a few hours. If it is very obstinate, rinse the jars free of all traces of bleach and put in a handful of fine gravel or coarse sand with a little water and swirl the jar so that the gravel scours in a rotary action. Always rinse jars thoroughly after any treatment of this sort and sterilize them as advised before use. This treatment is suitable for hard deposits or other matter difficult to remove.

Q. I have just taken the specific gravity of my finished wine and find that it is 1·000. Can I presume from this that I have made the maximum alcohol?

A. Only if you know the specific gravity you began with: as you did not tell me what this was I cannot help you. Always bear in mind that you must take the reading at the start if the reading at the end is to be of any use to you.

Q. I have been using sherry yeast and leaving the wine

exposed to air in the hope of making sherry but the wine while not quite finished has taken on the taste of vinegar. Is there anything I can do about this flavour or is the wine ruined.

A. The wine is ruined, I am sorry to say. Some people seem able to make sherry by the means you have tried – or so they say. But I have not found this method satisfactory.

Q. I have heard that the recipe for making marrow rum by taking the pips from a marrow and stuffing it with sugar is not satisfactory, yet I am told that people have made good marrow rum in this way. Would you let me have your valued opinion?

A. Whoever told you the marrow rum recipe you mention is not satisfactory was telling you the truth; the other people were not. The only stuff this recipe can turn out is a thick syrup which is quite unpalatable. All that can happen is that the inside of the marrow, being moist, dissolves the sugar, which leaves you with sugar diluted with marrow juice – nothing more.

Q. Is it possible to obtain yeast that will make wine as strong as port. If not, how is port made so strong?

A. You cannot obtain yeast to make wines as strong as port. The fact that port is a high alcohol wine is because it has been fortified with spirit.

Q. In all the books of yours that I have on this subject I have not known you to recommend using a corking machine. Is there any special reason for this?

A. There is. Years ago, when using one of these, a hairline crack invisible in the neck of the bottle opened up so that I had to have my hand stitched. This might have been my own fault for not examining the bottle thoroughly but one does not normally look for that sort of thing, though I suppose I should. At about this time, flanged corks became readily available as did the plastic seals with which to seal bottles, so I have used these ever since: and rather than recommend a corking machine to my readers who might have a similar accident, I advise flanged corks and plastic seals.

Q. I have been making wines for some time and have sent away for wine yeast. When I received them they were labelled as suitable for 1 to 5 gallons or 1 to 10 gallons depending on where I bought them. How much do I use for three gallons which is the size of most of my batches?

A. If you are making a starter you may use it all and apportion it between batches as necessary; if not, it may all be used for one batch. The amount of wine yeast added is not important provided there is enough at the start. Certainly there is no need at all to try to put what you might call an accurate amount in each batch.

Q. Is it in your opinion worthwhile to try to keep yeast for any length of time? I ask this because I have stored yeast in cool airy places, in the fridge and in cold dark places in the house and I have not had such good results from them as I have had from fresh supplies. In some cases the yeast had obviously deteriorated.

A. Good quality dried yeast should keep well for several months in dry airy conditions but, on the whole, most yeasts are so cheap and easy to get hold of that it hardly seems worthwhile storing if you seem to fail at this.

Here is a tip you might find useful if you make one batch straight after another or make one while another is already fermenting. Having prepared the new batch you may take a little of the deposit and a little of the wine from the fermenting batch to start off the new one. You only need a fluid ounce or so and this can be taken with the siphoning tube. If you are using special types of yeast suitable for certain types of wines you will have to be choosey but if your yeast is the popular general purpose yeast it may be used for all varieties of wines.

Q. I have an old recipe for fruit wine which says the fruits should be crushed and covered with water and allowed to stand until a thick mould forms on top . . .

A. Burn that recipe and forget you ever read it.

Q. Two of my fermentation locks are stained on the inside and one coated with flecks of yeast which was left when an over-vigorous fermentation forced some of the froth into them. Can you tell me how I can get rid of this trouble?

A. Either soak them in a mild solution of unscented soapless detergent such as Brobat or run a pipe cleaner through them. Rinse free of all detergent before use.

Q. I have often heard that filtering wine is the most suitable means of getting it brilliantly clear and I now feel that if I do not filter my wines they will not be really finished. Would you say that you recommended filtering or not?

A. I do not recommend filtering any wine. First of all, a well-made wine made with a suitable method and recipe will clear to brilliance unaided either by clarifiers or filtering. A wine made with a poor recipe or method that does not clear can be cleared with clarifiers when the trouble is known, ie, whether starch or pectin is causing the trouble. Bear in mind that the filtering will not clear wines where pectin or starch are present and filtering does, in the usual way, expose wine too long to the air and therefore there is a risk of over-oxydation.

Q. I would like to put a couple of bottles of my wines into the wine section of our local horticultural show. How is the best way to present the bottles?

A. Much depends on the requirements of your show organizers; their rules must be adhered to otherwise you may be disqualified. Much depends, too, on whether they issue much in the way of instructions as to how bottles should be presented. The larger shows give clear and concise instructions and issue their own labels, but smaller shows, where the wine section is, alas, often merely a space filler, merely invite exhibits, leaving the exhibitor with no idea of what is required. As yours is a local horticultural show, the wine section may come into this category.

Either way, scour your bottles inside and out with coarse sand or gravel and rinse thoroughly. Use clear glass punted bottles, no matter what colour the wine you are exhibiting. Punted bottles are those with the bottom pushed up inside.

Only brilliantly clear wine is good enough and there must be no suggestion of a hazy deposit in the bottle. Fill to one third of the way up the neck and finish off with a new cork of the flanged type. Polish the outside of the bottle when you have finished and do not finger it afterwards. Wrap in tissue and hold by the neck as you unwrap it.

If you have to put on a label of your own, make it a neat strip of white gummed paper just large enough to carry any writing that may be necessary. This may be type of wine or merely your exhibit number, depending on the requirements, or otherwise, of your show organizers. Best of luck!

Q. I have seen certain types of juice extractors offered to winemakers. Would these be of help in winemaking?

A. Some people use them but most do well without. Your best plan is to get hold of a set of directions for use and a price list and then decide whether you want to spend so much money or not.

Q. I have a number of solid rubber bungs, that is not the sort with holes in for fermentation locks. Would these be suitable to fit to jars of wine put away for storing? They do not smell of rubber in any way.

A. You did say storing, so I take it that you mean after the period required for oxydation. If fitted earlier these would not admit desired oxygen, so your wines would not improve by maturing.

In any case, if you have used rubber bungs with fitted fermentation locks you will have noticed how these take a mighty grip to the inside of the neck of the jar. The longer they remain undisturbed the harder they bind. For this reason, I think it would be risky to use them. I say this because, no matter how you may try, you will most likely have a batch of wine you thought had finished completely that will begin to ferment again.

If this happens, the rubber bung may be so tightly welded that it cannot blow out. The result would be that the jar would explode and if you happened to be near at hand at the time I shudder to think how badly you might be lacerated. After all, the pressure that can build up in a jar when sealed in this fashion is enormous, and the stronger the jar the more dangerous the explosion would be.

Q. I am using the plastic seals you recommended to give my wines that perfect finished appearance and to effect a perfect airtight seal. Would these allow the cork to blow out if, by some chance, some of my wine started fermenting again in the bottles? I am only worried because the seals become so tight a fit.

A. No need to worry, though I must say that this is a question worth asking. You will find, I am sure, that if your wines do start fermenting in the bottle, a certain amount of the wine will moisten the seal and therefore make it release its grip before the corks blow. Indeed, you will find this fact a useful guide as to whether you have any wines fermenting in bottle or not, so you can make a periodic inspection if you want to.

Q. I have several jars of brilliantly clear wine ready for sealing for long storing. But I find that there are a few small solids floating on the surface. As these are just under the beginning of the shoulders of the jar I cannot hook them out. I do not want to siphon the wine into other jars unless I have to. Do you know how I can remove these solids?

A. You did not say what these solids are but I take it that they might be harmful in some way if left in the wine.

The only means of removing these is to add a little of the same wine or a very similar wine to the affected jars so that the solids come into the necks where they may be taken off with the handle of a teaspoon. If they are solids that can be broken by doing this, you would do better to add sufficient wine to overflow them out of the jars altogether.

Q. I have some wine which has the unmistakable smell of yeast. How can I get rid of it?

A. I don't think you will rid the wine of this odour, but the remedy in future is to use a good yeast.

Q. While on holiday in Sussex I met an old chap nearing eighty who makes a lot of wine and he told me that he never uses yeast but puts in a hazel twig. He also told me that other people he knows use a hawthorn twig and they seem to make as good a wine as he does.

On trying to obtain further information from the old boy such as how these twigs could possibly have the same effect as good yeast he immediately fell silent as if there were some mystery about it to which he had been sworn to silence.

Naturally, being rather modern in outlook and having read a little about winemaking, I am a bit sceptical, and am wondering if you can tell me anything about the value of these twigs as yeast substitutes.

A. I am not surprised that the old gentleman went silent. It is probably that he got hold of this twig business in his early days and like most others years ago merely followed old wives' tales by the dozen when making wines. Another typical old wives' tale is that when wines that were bunged down as finished wines began to ferment again in the spring it was because they had become restless owing to the sap of the tree the fruits were taken from was rising again. What piffle! We know that wines made in late summer will stop fermenting owing to cold and because of this begin again when the weather turns warm in spring. So we make sure this does not happen by giving our fermenting wines warmth.

The twig business probably started when, quite accidentally, a twig of either trees mentioned happened to fall into the must. And the first thing noticed was that it was fermenting. So, of course, the twig got the credit for the fermentation.

Coming as I do from a long line of winemakers I have heard of much twaddle associated with this hobby and thank heaven we know better than to take notice of it.

Q. In your magazine articles and in other books of yours that I have, you nearly always end your instructions by recommending readers to fill the jar to where the neck begins. I do this, of course, but what puzzles me is that if I fill the jar at this stage I find later that more space is made as more of the sugar is used up during fermentation but there is no instruction to fill the jar to where the neck begins again. Why fill the jar once and not later when there is a little more space left that could be filled?

A. You are not the first to ask about this and I do not expect you to be the last. When you fill the jar to where the neck begins you use the final addition of the total amount of water required in relation to the amount of fruit and sugar used for the type of wine being made. If later on when the yeast has used up a little more sugar and the level of the wine falls slightly you were to add more water, you would dilute the flavour and the alcohol and the desired final sweetness of the wine. The yeast would make up the alcohol and in so doing use up more sugar and so make a drier wine than you want.

When this happened, you would find a little more space left in the jar and if you filled up again you would merely repeat the process. So filling the jar to where the neck begins once and once only is important.

Q. I must admit that your modern methods give far better results than I have ever had from using those handed on by my parents. But what puzzles me is that you never include in your recipes methods making enough wine to have a little left over for what my mother called topping up. She used to top up the jars every day with some of the wine made for the purpose. When making a batch of say three gallons, she used to make about an extra half gallon. This was kept separate and the jars filled to the brim every day so that there was always a little to overflow down the sides of the jar. There were no such things as fermentation locks in those days but she always finished up with a jar filled to the brim whether she was making a three-gallon lot or a five-gallon one.

Would you say it might be a good idea, now that fermentation locks protect our wines, to make just a little extra, say an extra pint or so, so that instead of having just under a gallon when the wine is finished, we would have a complete gallon?

A. Topping up is still widely practised even though fermentation locks protect our wines. The odd part about this operation in old methods was that it was supposed to prevent bacteria reaching the wine yet the tops of the jars were left uncovered. It is a fact that during the vigorous fermentation stage a cloud of gas from fermentation would hang in the neck of the jar to prevent contamination but this would not be the case when fermentation slowed down. And it was at this stage that old methods recommended 'popping the corks in loosely'. Loose corking allowed all sorts of bacteria and wild yeasts to gain access and spoil the wine.

If you want to be certain of a whole gallon when fermentation has ceased, you may certainly make a little more than a gallon by increasing the ingredients and water proportionately.

And then when fermentation reduces the level in the jar, top up with the excess. This little extra should be kept in a small bottle plugged tightly with cotton wool.

Alternatively, it might be better to make two-gallon lots. And then when fermentation has ceased, fill a one-gallon jar and a half-gallon jar and bottle the remainder.

You will appreciate that to include this sort of instruction in all the recipes and methods would be more than most readers could put up with, especially as this topping-up operation is more the choice of the hobbyist than a necessity.

Q. I have read in various places that one should add ammonium sulphate, magnesium sulphate, potassium phosphate and other chemicals if you want to obtain good results in winemaking, yet I cannot find any trace of these included in any recipe I have or in the books of yours that I have.

Will you please tell me whether these chemicals are necessary or not. If they are, how much of each would be needed for a gallon of wine?

A. The reason you do not find these chemicals mentioned, as such, in modern books is because these are contained in most nutrients in balanced quantities. Years ago when there were no manufactured nutrient tablets or powders on the market many people used to make up their own nutrient with the chemicals you mention together with others. This is not necessary today. The various nutrients available today are cheap, convenient and easy to handle and carefully blended to give the required balance between the various chemicals.

Q. Do you think it would be worthwhile trying to revive interest in what we used to call Bee Wine? All I can remember about this is that some sort of yeast was mixed with sugar and water. The result was supposed to be something like ginger beer. I think we used to call it ginger beer plant, or Californian bees.

A. As I have had to explain about the so-called Marrow Rum, this recipe for ginger beer plant, or whatever you care to call it, is not worth a second thought. I realize that this caused some sort of fascination many years ago – indeed, I can recall as a child my elder brothers having a bottle of it in the sunshine of the kitchen window. Lumps of 'something' were floating up and down with the upsurge of gas caused by fermentation but I know for certain that it never came to anything worth having.

A few years ago, someone started off the idea in a national newspaper calling it the ginger beer plant. My name accidentally became mixed up with it and I was inundated with letters about this for weeks afterwards. And weeks later came hundreds of complaints. How glad I was to be able to explain that it was not my idea in the first place.

Q. I have your book *Home Winemaking* and I must say how all the photos make everything so clear that the instructions are so easy to follow.

But one thing puzzles me. When I put wine into a jar, the solution in the lock begins to bubble at once. Then perhaps later on, I find that the solution, instead of being pushed up on the out-going side, is drawn up on the wrong side. That is, it appears that air is about to be drawn into the jar. Could you explain what is happening?

A. This is not really a problem and it need not worry you. A vigorous ferment such as when the wine is first put into a jar will cause the solution to be pushed up on the outgoing side and bubbles of gas will be seen passing through this. Later, as this vigorous ferment slows, some loss of natural warmth caused by yeast activity is lost so that the wine shrinks (contracts), thus leaving a small air-space in the jar. And because this must be made up, air is drawn in. Hence your noticing that the solution is drawn up on the wrong side.

This also happens sometimes when a change of temperature is allowed to affect the wine such as when constant warmth at a given temperature cannot be maintained. The temperature change affects the volume of the wine in the jar so that the amount of air overhead varies. In case you are bothered as to when fermentation has ceased while you are having this trouble, just leave everything as it is because when fermentation has ceased, the solution will slowly return to level in the 'U' bend of the lock and remain there.

Q. I have read and been told that before one can hope to

make good wines one must be able to use what is known as acidemetric apparatus in order to obtain a chemically balanced wine. The writer and those who told me make it all sound so simple and convince me that this is necessary. Now, I have made some wines with your *Home Winemaking* and I must admit that these really are good wines. Would they be *all that* much better if I learned to use and then used this acidemetric apparatus?

A. No, they would not. And if you did learn to use this chemical apparatus which is a difficult thing to do if you do not happen to have attained a certain standard of academic knowledge both in chemistry and mathematics, it is doubtful whether your wines would be any better than they are when made from reliable recipes. Common sense application of recipes and methods and the insight and judgement needed to alter a recipe slightly in order to obtain slightly different results are likely to give you far better results than using all the scientific and chemical apparatus that a lot of people would like to see amateurs clutter themselves with.

Winemaking is essentially a simple hobby with a chemical background. Some knowledge of this background is needed and will certainly be found in most modern books – including this one. Keeping winemaking simple makes it a pleasant and rewarding hobby. Making it expensive and brain-taxing will only rob it of its interest and pleasure.

The fact that you have already made good wine with the recipes in my other books should be evidence that simplicity of recipe and method gives amply good results.

Q. I have heard that it is essential that bottles be thoroughly dried before wine is put into them. This seems odd to me but a friend who used to make wine tells me she used to bake them in an oven. She has now given up winemaking mainly because she often cracked the bottles or burned herself.

A. I have heard of this practice but I think the idea behind it was to sterilize the bottles. This certainly sounds like something from Granny's winemaking era.

When sterilizing bottles as we do these days with sterilizing solution, there is absolutely no need at all to dry them though naturally it is wise to let them drain for a moment or two.

Q. I have been using your recipes and methods for many years now and almost always with the best possible results. But nearly always I get a vigorous fermentation immediately after putting the wine into the jar. For this reason I plug the neck with cotton wool for a few days before fitting the lock. This is a precaution I take because quite often I have had this vigorous fermentation push froth into the lock and even right through and over the top so that it ran down the side of the jar.

Other winemakers I have talked to do not experience this, even those who use your recipes and methods. Indeed, some say that fermentation is very slow for a week or so after it is put into a jar.

Can you explain why I have this bother?

A. I see that you have found your own sensible answer to this problem. Some people do have this sort of thing happen. It is often caused by warmth while transferring to the jar or by giving the yeast an airing. Either of these would start a vigorous fermentation and the two combined would make it even more vigorous. Another factor is that you may be using a different yeast to your friends. But very often little problems like these are peculiar to an individual operator.

If this problem persists, it would be wise to leave your wines in the fermenting vessel for a day or two longer as it could be that the fermentation in the vessel is not as vigorous as it should be. My directions to put the wine into a gallon jar after a certain time in the fermentation vessel are on the assumption that your wines will react in the same manner as most others, so that by the time you put yours into a jar the vigorous ferment is over and that only a slow fermentation will go on inside the jar. Local conditions will, of course, put out various calculations but generally – as your friends confirm – my directions are best for the majority.

Chapter 23

FINAL WORDS WITH A FEW NOTES FOR OVERSEAS READERS

When you are making wines you will meet all sorts of people who will try to persuade you against your chosen course. They will try to convince you that such and such is no good or that this and that is much better. They quote from either their own or the experience of others but what they overlook is that what they or their friends do or the results they obtain from whatever it is that they do suits them and they expect it to suit you as well. It is rather like having someone tell you that the film at the local cinema is absolutely terrific. In their eyes it might be, but the chances are that if you went along yourself, you would wonder what on earth your friends had raved over.

Winemaking is essentially a very personal hobby. You are yourself, working as you want to, just as you would clean and tidy your own house or maintain your garden. I can imagine your reaction if someone started to tell you how you ought to be doing these things. Yet when making wines, people are inclined to be led astray very often by people who know very little about the subject but who talk about it in such a convincing manner and very often put themselves over so well that the poor listener is filled with doubts as to whether he is doing the right thing or not.

I was with another well-known winemaker at a meeting some time ago and we offered a rather talkative chap some of our wines. Having sampled them and praised them up to the point where he would not let himself go further simply because he wanted to tell us all about winemaking, he started off. If he had made this he would have done so and so but then doing that would have altered this and so on and so on.

We listened until a member of the club we were visiting came over and introduced us. The poor chap! I can still see his face. However, we quickly put him at ease and we are now good friends.

I think this is important in winemaking. Making friends enables you to share experiences and talk about wines and winemaking generally. But when you have learned about winemaking you will be able to identify at once those who know a lot about the subject and those who just kid you along that they do.

You will learn more about winemaking than this book will teach you because there is still a lot being learned about the subject. It is rather like medicine and surgery, the doctors of the world are still learning how to understand the new techniques and the use of new drugs.

Although we think we understand winemaking, we do not. We only understand what is on the surface. Underneath, there are scientific principles that are far from understood. Even the relatively simple process of fermentation is, in reality, so complicated and involved that scientists do not fully understand what goes on or why it goes on.

But what we do know is sufficient to allow us to make first-class wines and this book will show you all you will need to know for a lifetime of pleasure, not only in having an interesting and rewarding hobby, but also in being able to build yourself a very valuable cellar full of excellent products. But you will not be able to do this if you listen to a cascade of differing views and opinions and recommendations.

So now we are back where we began. Choose your course and then stick to it. You will not regret it, I assure you.

American readers wondering how best to alter these recipes to suit their gallon – which is different to the British Imperial gallon – will bear in mind that they can make five-gallon lots where all they have to do is to use four times the amount of ingredients I recommend for one gallon and then use five American gallons of water.

For the benefit of my American friends and readers and especially members of the Bravery Winemaking Club of

America, let me just say that the sultanas mentioned in some of these recipes are known to you as white raisins.

Further, those of you who want to make wines with huckle-berries will do very well if you follow the recipes for black-berries.

Those of you who will be looking for supplies of yeast and nutrients and perhaps other things will find the addresses of suppliers in your country at the end of this book.

And now I would like to wish all my readers all over the world – Happy Winemaking!

Appendix I

COMPARISON OF PERCENTAGE OF ALCOHOL BY VOLUME AND DEGREES OF PROOF

The term 'proof spirit' is an antiquated description of the alcohol content of wines and spirits. Actually, the proof spirit content is most misleading because it gives the impression to the average person that a spirit of 75° means that it contains 75 parts per 100 parts (75 per cent) pure alcohol, whereas it does not. Gin for example with a proof spirit content of 70° actually contains 40 parts per 100 of pure alcohol or, in other words, 40 per cent of alcohol by volume. Measuring the alcohol content as by volume is by far the most accurate means.

Alcohol by volume per cent means that if a wine is 15 per cent of alcohol by volume, 15 parts of each 100 parts is pure alcohol. In other words, if you were to divide whatever amount of wine you might have into 100 parts and the alcohol could be separated, 15 parts of the 100 would be pure alcohol. The 40 per cent by volume gin just mentioned would produce 40 parts of each 100 as pure alcohol. It will be seen from this that per cent proof is quite misleading.

However, most of you will want to know how your alcohol by volume compares with proof spirit and the table below will show you the range wide enough to cover the various degrees of alcohol content that you may be producing in your wines.

Alcohol by Volume per cent	Degrees Proof Spirit
8	13·9
9	15·6
10	17·4
11	19·3
12	21·6
13	22·7
14	24·5
15	26·2
16	28·0

Appendix II

COMPARISON TABLE OF DEGREES FAHRENHEIT AND CENTIGRADE

It will be seen that certain temperatures are mentioned in various parts of this book and that these are given as F. = Fahrenheit. But as we have now changed to C. = Centigrade, this comparison table will be found useful. This is not a complete table but covers sufficiently the range of figures you are likely to come across when making wine and beer.

F.	Represents	C.
71·6		22
69·8		21
68·0		20
66·2		19
64·4		18
62·6		17
60·8		16
59·0		15
57·2		14
55·4		13
53·6		12
51·8		11
50·0		10
48·2		9
46·4		8
44·6		7
42·8		6
41·0		5
39·2		4
37·4		3
35·6		2
33·8		1
32·0		0 Freezing

SUPPLIERS

Fermenta, 58–60 Kingston Road, New Malden, Surrey: yeasts, nutrient, special flavourings, and T'noirot extracts.

Joseph Bryant, 95 Old Market Street, Bristol 2: all utensils, yeasts and concentrates.

Semplex, Old Hall Works, Stuart Road, Higher Tranmere, Birkenhead, Cheshire.

W. R. Loftus Ltd, 1–3 Charlotte Street, London W1: everything for the home winemakers but for personal shoppers only.

W. R. Loftus Ltd, 16 The Terrace, Torquay: mail order only; everything for the home winemaker.

Winemaker's Equipment Ltd, 242 Deansgate, Manchester 3: everything for the home winemaker.

Home Winemaker's Supplies, 6 Withy Grove, Manchester 4: everything for the home winemaker.

Leigh-Williams and Sons, 9 Eastern Drive, Grassendale, Liverpool 19: everything for the home winemaker.

Southern Vineyards, 28 Crescent Road, Brighton, Sussex, BN2 3RP: concentrated grape juices, yeasts, and nutrients.

Vinaide, 28 Swan Street, Manchester 4: all requirements of the home winemaker and home brewer.

Vinaide, Alfred Street, Central, Nottingham: everything for the home winemaker and home brewer.

Rogers (Mead) Ltd, 27 Vicarage Road, Wednesfield, Staffs.: yeasts, nutrients, dried fruit, scales and balances.

Home Brewing Centre, 120 Pinner Road, Harrow, Middlesex: all home brewing requirements.

Continental Wine Experts, The Winery, North Walsham, Norfolk: yeasts, nutrient, dried fruits, fruit pulps, essences and flavourings.

The 'House of Bacchus', 5 The Corridor, Market Place, Leicester: most requirements of the home winemaker.

Note: Prices vary with each firm and postage is expensive, so it pays to shop around and near home: send for several price lists and compare prices.

Overseas Suppliers
Canada. Wine Art, PO BOX 2701, Vancouver 3, B.C.: all requirements.

USA. Aetna Bottle Co Inc, 708 Rainer Avenue South, Seattle 44, Washington: all requirements.

New Zealand. Brewers Trading Co, PO BOX 593, Christchurch, New Zealand: all requirements. This firm also serves Australia.

INDEX

Notes